RISE ABOVE IT:

FIVE POWERFUL STRATEGIES FOR OVERCOMING ADVERSITY AND ACHIEVING SUCCESS

DONNA DAISY PH.D.
WITH ABBY DONNELLY

Trafford Publishing

Cover design: Ruth Kuttler
Typesetting and design: Ruth Kuttler, Advanced Internet & Design Concepts

Printed in Victoria, Canada

National Library of Canada Cataloguing in Publication

Daisy, Donna
  Rise above it: five powerful strategies for overcoming
adversity and achieving success / Donna Daisy, Abby Donnelly.
ISBN 1-55369-359-0
  1. Success--Psychological aspects. I. Donnelly, Abby II.
Title.
BF637.S8D33 2002   158.1   C2002-901409-3

This book was published *on-demand* in cooperation with Trafford Publishing.
On-demand publishing is a unique process and service of making a book available for retail sale to the public taking advantage of on-demand manufacturing and Internet marketing. **On-demand publishing** includes promotions, retail sales, manufacturing, order fulfilment, accounting and collecting royalties on behalf of the author.

Suite 6E, 2333 Government St., Victoria, B.C. V8T 4P4, CANADA
Phone   250-383-6864   Toll-free   1-888-232-4444 (Canada & US)
Fax   250-383-6804   E-mail   sales@trafford.com
Web site   www.trafford.com   TRAFFORD PUBLISHING IS A DIVISION OF TRAFFORD HOLDINGS LTD.
Trafford Catalogue #02-0172   www.trafford.com/robots/02-0172.html

10   9   8   7   6   5   4

Table of Contents

i

TABLE OF CONTENTS

TABLE OF CONTENTS

iv

ACKNOWLEDGMENTS

Our deepest thanks to the many friends who have supported us in this endeavor. Special thanks to Ruth Kuttler for her excellence in layout, design, and graphic art, and for her diligence and commitment to our efforts; to Karen Olander for her amazing patience and tremendous assistance with editing (no small task), and the staff of Trafford Publishing for pulling it all together and making this book a reality.

From Donna, deep appreciation to my children, David, Kathy, and Kim, who have put up with my many personal growth stages, which, at times, probably seemed a little unusual; to my parents, who unfailingly believed in me; to my sister, Carol, who has always been there for me, and most of all to my husband, Charles, who never fails to light the way with his love, patience and support. Special thanks to Abby Donnelly, outstanding coach and trainer, always steadfast even in times of discouragement. Thank you for believing in this project, and encouraging me, first as my coach, now as my partner.

From Abby, to my parents, Ellen and Lawrence Danziger, who lived by the financial principles outlined in this book, you gave me the foundation to live my passion; to my dear friend and partner, Donna, this book reflects your knowledge, insight, and passion for helping others be incredibly successful. I am so honored to have been a part of it. To my husband, Jim, my biggest champion and my wisest counsel, you taught me about the power to choose, and you were the best choice I ever made.

● ●

RISE ABOVE IT:

FIVE POWERFUL STRATEGIES FOR OVERCOMING ADVERSITY AND ACHIEVING SUCCESS

Section I
Introduction

Have you ever noticed that some people are incredibly successful in whatever they try to do? Life appears so easy for them. Other people seem to barely get by, often stopping short of their goals, or giving up completely. Things don't always go as well for these people and life is always a struggle. What are the differences between these people?

Think about yourself. Are there areas of your life where you are remarkably successful, and other areas in which things just never seem to go right?

- Maybe it is in relationships.
- Maybe it is with finances.
- Maybe it is in your career.

1

As a Success Coach, I often talk with people who are disappointed with their lack of success in their career, or who are experiencing phenomenal success at work, but are disappointed in their personal lives. I have found myself wondering, "Are there basic differences between people who achieve the results they want in their lives and have a successful, fulfilling life, and those who rarely attain their goals and have just an average or even a disappointing life? If so, what are those differences?"

In 1994 Dr. George Pransky and Dr. Roger Mills first introduced me to the concept that there is a line that separates those who are phenomenally successful and happy in their lives from those who are unsuccessful at achieving their goals, unfulfilled, and unhappy. In a workshop called Health Realization, they taught that fulfillment and happiness—even success—are determined by how people use their minds, what they focus on and how they think about events in their lives, all of which determines how they respond to those events. For example, when moving to a new city due to the relocation of their company, "above the line" people would notice the beautiful garden areas, the outstanding school system, the fine restaurants, and other qualities that made the city attractive. These people would be enthusiastic and happy about moving to that city. The "below the line" people would be likely to respond by focusing on the one run-down neighborhood and the city dump, and they would be miserable about moving to that particular city. Pransky and Mills also shared the determining factors for living above or below that line, and then taught strategies that can help people choose to live above the line.

A few years later, I attended a seminar at the Harvard Institute of Mind/Body Medicine where we reviewed key research findings on stress and its impact on our lives. I learned that, when faced with stress and/or adversity, some people are inclined to feel helpless and give up, and others persevere toward their goals. The concept of "the line" was expanded to include a line that divides those people who feel empowered in life from those who feel helpless.

An example of this concept is the story of several participants of a support group for women who had recently undergone mastectomies. The women in the group had very different responses. The one who felt helpless said, "My whole life is ruined. I'm so ugly that nobody will ever love me again." The woman became more and more unhappy and lacking in self-confidence, eventually isolating herself completely from the people in her life that she cared most about. Another woman dramatically empowered herself with her attitude: "I may not be perfect, but parts of me are excellent, and I'm going to enjoy my life!"

In 1998, I was introduced to still another "line" in a book called "The OZ Principle," written by authors Roger Connors, Tom Smith, and Craig Hickman. They referred to a line that divides great results from poor results, outstanding companies from mediocre companies, winners from losers. They then described the characteristics of those who operated above the line. One illustration of this is a major corporation that assigned new projects to two teams within the company. The response of one team

4

leader to the project was "I don't know why they chose this project. It doesn't have a chance of succeeding and will take way too much of our time." The response of another team leader was, "Don't tell us why it won't work. Let us figure out how it *can* work." You can imagine which team had a successful project completion!

By this time, it had become very clear to me that if a person was living "below the line," the name of the game is **"RISE ABOVE IT."** It was less clear exactly how to do that.

As I began my research for my doctoral dissertation, I confirmed that there are definite and distinguishable differences between those who give up and those who succeed. These differences have very little to do with luck, as some of us think, and everything to do with how we respond to adversity and to life's challenges. The key to success is having:

- **a mindset that promotes resilience in times of adversity,**
- **life skills that enhance effective responses to life's challenges, and**

5

- **lifestyle that will allow you to maintain the success you achieve.**

Most of us have dreams and goals we want to achieve in our lives. If things always went smoothly, we would all achieve those goals and see our dreams become a reality. But life has a way of throwing obstacles in our path. Those who are unprepared to handle challenges and adversity will become frustrated, discouraged, and are likely to give up long before their goals are achieved. Those who are resilient and equipped with life skills that allow them to be effective in their responses to challenges will keep trying even in the most difficult of times—and, they are likely to succeed!

The landmark work of many top researchers such as Martin Seligman and Suzanne Oullette has made it clear that managing stress and adversity and achieving success don't happen by accident. People who succeed are not necessarily experiencing less adversity than those who fail. They simply have what it takes to **RISE ABOVE IT.** They have acquired the necessary mindset and skills to respond effectively when the going gets tough. Almost without exception, researchers support this key premise:

> "It is not *what* happens to us that separates success from failure. It is **how we *perceive* what** happens and *how we respond* that makes the difference."

Successful people use specific strategies that allow them to respond effectively and support their ability to get the results they want. If you want to achieve success in your life—whatever success means to you—it is essential for you to be in control of how you respond to negative events in your life. Taking control of how you respond to adversity requires knowing at a deep level that you always have the choice of how you will respond and that your choice of responses will ultimately determine whether you succeed or fall short of achieving your goals.

This book will provide the knowledge and strategies you need to respond to life's challenges in a way that will allow you to:

- overcome stress and adversity
- achieve success, and
- sustain success.

It explains the fine line that separates success from failure, having an incredible life from having just an "O.K." life. The *line* represents the adversity that occurs in your life. People who function above the line are empowered and effective. People who function below the line are more inclined to feel helpless, like victims of their circumstances. What I am going to share with you in this book will give you the tools to **RISE ABOVE IT** and stay there consistently.

I often find that something visual is helpful in "getting" certain concepts. The following is a good illustration for what we accomplish when we **"RISE ABOVE IT."**

SUCCESS

THE ADVERSITY LINE: RISE ABOVE IT

FAILURE

Where do you place yourself on this illustration? Does adversity get the better of you, causing you to fall below the fine, or are you resilient enough to rise above that line and move toward the success you want in your life?

We know that there are identifiable differences between people who succeed in achieving their goals and those who fail. Section I of this book provides the research-based understanding of those differences and a clear model for developing a strong personal foundation for achieving the success you want in your life. The components that I identify as essential for a strong personal foundation are:

9

- A Mindset of Hardiness
- Life Skills for Effectiveness, and
- A Lifestyle of Self-care that supports success.

In today's challenging environment of change and uncertainty, it is more important than ever that each of us have the strategies and skills we need to withstand adversity in order to achieve the success and fulfillment we want in our lives. The good news is that you can learn to respond in a productive way to stress and adversity and increase your personal and professional effectiveness. **Section II** of this book gives you five powerful strategies that will

> *"The good news is that you can learn to respond in a productive way to stress and adversity and increase personal effectiveness."*

allow you to overcome adversity and make your dreams a reality. These strategies are grounded in research, and are combined with many practical tools for achieving your personal and professional goals. By applying these strategies in your life on a daily basis, you will quickly strengthen your ability to:

- respond constructively to adversity,

- improve your overall effectiveness, and
- make consistent progress toward making your vision for your life a reality.

When adversity occurs, you always have a choice. You can become helpless and give up, believing that nothing you do will make a difference. Or, you can choose to become empowered by acquiring the mindset, the lifestyle, and the life skills that will allow you to:

- take control of your life and keep it,
- be resilient in times of adversity, and
- develop the effectiveness you need to consistently move forward on your path to success.

It is my hope that as you read this book, you will come to better understand the incredible power of your mindset, your life skills, and your lifestyle as they influence your ability to **RISE ABOVE IT.** More important, as you incorporate the empowering mindset, lifestyle, and life skills into your life, you will quickly begin to see exciting results.

You may find that the best way to use this book is to first read it all the way through to get a grasp of the overall message. Then go back and gradually start putting the strategies into action in your life.

Learning and change are often easier and more powerful when shared with a friend. One approach is to read a section, then discuss it together. Share with each other the strategies you are implementing, and celebrate together as you start experiencing the positive changes that put you on the road to achieving the success and fulfillment that you want in your life.

If you want to enjoy the phenomenal experience of living above that line that separates empowerment from helplessness, great results from poor results, and success from failure, take advantage of the information in this book. Learn how you can RISE ABOVE IT and enjoy more success and fulfillment in your life, starting now!

Model For Success

1

A s I was completing my doctoral studies, I realized that my research had provided the makings of a powerful Model for Success. It became very clear to me that the ability to achieve the results we want in our lives often depends on how resilient we are in the face of adversity. One of the biggest challenges we all face in our lives is continuing to work toward our goals when life throws obstacles in our paths, or when we just get discouraged. For me, writing this book is a good example of that kind of situation. Some days I just couldn't seem to find the right words to make a key point, and I would wonder if I even had what it takes to write a book. I was pretty comfortable with my life without having written a book, so I would find myself asking, "Why am I putting myself through this?" But something deep inside me kept me going. I knew I had what it takes to rise above my self-doubt. I had set a goal that I was deeply committed to, and I was not going to let discouragement get the best of me. I knew I had the mindset, knowledge base, perseverance, and skill I needed to turn my dream (this book) into a reality— and I did it!

We Need a Sense of Control

No matter what our goals are, we need the sense of control that comes from consciously choosing how we will respond to any discouragement or adversity that comes our way. We also need a strong belief in our ability to respond effectively to life's challenges. Otherwise, we are likely to become discouraged very quickly, and give up long before we achieve our goals.

People gain a sense of control and belief in their own effectiveness when they have a strong personal foundation of beliefs, skills, and lifestyle that promotes resilience and effectiveness.

> *"People gain a sense of control when they have a strong personal foundation."*

With a strong personal foundation, we are well prepared to get rid of old ways of doing things

14

that aren't working very well for us, and installing some new and more effective approaches for getting the results we want.

The Model for Success

Based on research on learned helplessness, stress hardiness, goal achievement, and other key findings, I created a model that provides the philosophy and the tools you need to build that strong personal foundation for responding to adversity in a constructive way and consistently getting the results you want. I call this the *Model for Success*.

A Mindset of Hardiness

Model For Success

Life Skills For Effectiveness

Lifestyle of Self-Care

The model consists of three components:
1. A Mindset of Hardiness
2. Life Skills for Effectiveness, and
3. A Lifestyle of Self-Care.

A Mindset of Hardiness is essential for increasing resilience—the ability to bounce back from adversity. The Life Skills for Effectiveness allow you to take necessary actions to achieve success. The third component—Lifestyle of Self-Care—provides the means of supporting and maintaining success.

The model provides the framework of understanding needed to build a strong personal foundation for developing powerful and effective responses to adversity. The strategies that accompany the model provide the mechanism for putting the principles of the model to work in your own life. They give you the skills for taking control of your life, strengthening your resilience, and achieving personal and professional success.

In my own life, when I am learning new skills for effectiveness, I find it helpful first to develop a clear understanding of the principles behind the strategies I am adopting. When I am clear about why I am using a particular strategy, my commitment to the implementation of that strategy and belief in its potential effectiveness is much stronger. For that reason, it was important to me that the Model for Success be grounded in solid, research-based understandings of human motivation, personal effectiveness (self-efficacy), resilience to stress and adversity, and goal setting and achievement. But it was equally important that the strategies supporting the model be down to earth and user-friendly.

The model that I have developed is a powerful, yet easy-to-apply method for taking control of your life and getting the results you want by:

- getting clear about what success looks like for you (the results you want),
- developing a strong commitment to that success,
- strengthening your resilience to stress and adversity,
- building the life skills you need for personal and professional success, and
- maintaining a lifestyle that supports and sustains your success.

As I developed the model, and began applying what I had learned in my own life, I also began encouraging

17

my coaching clients to do the same. The results were incredible! As my clients became clear about the results they wanted in their lives, and gained confidence in their ability to take charge of their lives, they were able to deal more effectively with adversity and keep moving forward toward their goals. They experienced one success after another. Their relationships became healthier. Business results also flourished as they became more focused and prioritized where they wanted to direct their energy. But another amazing thing occurred for almost everyone who began to understand the concepts behind the model and to apply the strategies. They found that, when faced with a difficult situation, the *process* of dealing effectively with that challenge became almost as great a source of satisfaction and accomplishment as the actual attainment of the original goal. They were so bolstered by their own ability to overcome problems and keep moving forward toward their goals that their self-confidence increased tremendously. As their self-confidence increased, so did their success in reaching their goals. These positive results, both in my own life and in that of my clients, led to my desire to share with each of you the tools and methodologies found in this book.

Basic and Significant Differences

The Model for Success is based on the amazing discoveries made by many prominent researchers about some of the basic differences between people who are resilient in the face of stress and adversity, and keep striving toward the achievement of their goals, and those who become discouraged and give up. Researchers such as Martin Seligman point out that successful people tend to be optimistic instead of pessimistic. They feel they are in charge of their lives. Pessimists often see themselves as victims of their circumstances. Successful people typically view adversity and/or change as a challenge; others view these things as disastrous.

Whether we persist toward our goals and achieve the success we want, or become discouraged and fold under pressure often depends on the strength of our personal foundation. A strong personal foundation which is typical of highly effective

19

people includes each of the key components of the model:

- A Mindset of Hardiness with which we approach our goals and challenges,
- A high level of Life Skills for Effectiveness, and
- A Lifestyle of Self-Care that supports and sustains that success.

The Model for Success is based on the premise that it's not the circumstances of your life, but how you respond to those circumstances that matters. A friend of mind, Nancy, shared with me a perfect example of how this model worked in her life. At age 43, Nancy was discouraged by the circumstances in which she found herself. She was a single mom with three children to care for, working as a bank teller earning $7.50 an hour. But Nancy had a vision for her life. She also had a strong belief in herself and an optimistic outlook that prompted her to return to college and begin a

> *"The Model for Success is based on the premise that it's not the circumstances of your life, but how you respond to those circumstances that matters. "*

Master's Program. With incredible persistence, Nancy managed to get her tuition paid for and, in addition, she was offered a part-time job as an Academic Advisor. Even with an eleven-month-old baby and two teenagers, she juggled all the balls and graduated with honors two years later. At the age of 45, she earned her Master's Degree in Social Sciences.

As doors began to open and opportunities began to appear, Nancy grabbed them. While working as a therapist in a private psychiatric hospital, Nancy overheard a colleague say that she was going for a flying lesson. In Nancy's words, "My ears grew to the size of an elephant's ears. My brain exploded. I wanted—no I *had* to do that." So at age 50, Nancy began to learn how to fly. Learning to fly forced her past her comfort zone but it also provided another challenge and she was determined to succeed. Nancy believed in herself and her ability to rise to the challenge. Nancy successfully attained her pilot's license and now speaks of the perspective of the Earth from her cockpit which keeps her "grounded" and "able to see the face of God."

A fter attaining her pilot's license, Nancy was ready for yet another challenge. She had learned that doing what seemed impossible had brought wholeness and contentment, peace and sacredness into her life. For the next two years, she contemplated her next goal—pursuing her doctoral degree. At the age of 56, and with reservations as to whether or not her brain could really meet the task, she decided to "go for it." She began her doctoral program, and today, 2-½ years later, is awaiting the final approval of her dissertation. She did it! She rose to the challenge and is now looking for the next challenge.

Nancy definitely has the personal foundation necessary to overcome a situation she wasn't happy with and achieve the success she wanted in her life. There is no doubt that she has a mindset of hardiness (resilience). She worked diligently at acquiring the life skills she needed and, as she began reaching her goals, Nancy also began practicing a lifestyle of self-care (relaxation, healthy diet, regular exercise) that allows her to sustain the successes she has worked so hard to achieve.

Adversity, stress, and challenges are always present in our lives. The Model for Success and the strategies that accompany it give you the tools to build the strong personal foundation you need to rise above these difficulties in your life. By applying the concepts of the model and the strategies on a consistent basis, you will strengthen your ability to rise above your toughest challenges, keep moving toward your goals, and achieve the success that you want in your life.

A s is true for any model, there is a relationship of interdependence among the three constructs. The main component, a Mindset of Hardiness, is supported by acquiring and then consistently applying the Life Skills for Effectiveness, and creating and maintaining a Lifestyle of Self-Care that supports success. Each construct of the model is essential; they must work together at all times. When the three components are working together effectively, you have the tools you need to:

• Rise above stress and adversity **(RISE ABOVE IT)**,

- Increase the likelihood that you will persevere toward your goals, and
- Maximize your potential for success.

> *"When the components of the model are working together effectively, you have all the tools you need to successfully achieve your goals."*

IN A NUTSHELL

1. There are significant differences between people who are resilient and frequently successful in achieving their goals, and those who are less resilient and tend to give up more easily.

2. The ability to achieve the results you want in your life often depends on how resilient you are in the face of adversity.

3. No matter what your goals are, you need the sense of control that comes from consciously choosing how you will respond to any discouragement or adversity that comes your way.

4. Whether you persist toward your goals and achieve the success you want, or become

24

discouraged and fold under pressure often depends on the strength of your personal foundation.

5. You gain a sense of control and belief in your own effectiveness when you have a strong personal foundation of beliefs, skills, and lifestyle that promotes resilience and effectiveness.

6. The Model for Success, which includes a Mindset of Hardiness, Life Skills for Effectiveness, and Lifestyle of Self-Care, provides the philosophy and the tools you need to build that strong personal foundation for responding to adversity in a constructive way and consistently getting the results you want.

7. A Mindset of Hardiness is essential for increasing resilience.

8. The Life Skills for Effectiveness allow you to take necessary actions to achieve success.

9. The Lifestyle of Self-Care provides the means of supporting and maintaining success.

10. When all three components of the Model for Success are working together effectively, you

have all the tools you need to successfully achieve your goals.

11. The five strategies in Section II provide the specific tools and action steps that are necessary to consistently move toward the achievement of your goals.

• •

Foundations For Success:
From Helplessness to Empowerment

2

Most of us would agree that we want to be successful. We have hopes; we have dreams; and we have goals that we want to achieve. Success means different things to different people. Some define success in terms of how much money they make. Some define it in terms of job title. For others, the significant accumulation of material things such as a big house, a fancy car, or fine jewelry signals success. Still others say they will feel successful when they feel fulfilled. While each of us probably has some criteria of success in our minds, I like the definition of success put forth by Paul Stoltz in his book, *Adversity Quotient.* Stoltz defines success as "the degree to which one moves forward and upward, progressing in one's lifelong mission, despite all obstacles or other forms of adversity." Note that the emphasis is on the *process* of moving toward your goals, not on a final product.

A Fly in the Ointment

Even though you may be very clear about what success means to you, life often has a way of putting a fly in the ointment. Obstacles are thrown in our path. Adversity happens! I define adversity as "any situation or event that has the potential to discourage you and/or get in the way of achieving your goals." When you are striving toward a goal, and run into

> *"Adversity is any situation or event that has the potential to discourage you or get in the way of your goals."*

challenges and discouraging situations, the key to whether you will keep trying and ultimately achieve your goal, or get discouraged and give up often lies in how well you manage stress and adversity. When you feel that you have no control over a stressful situation,

> *"The key to whether you succeed or give up often lies in how well you manage stress and adversity."*

or that there is nothing you can do that will make any difference to the outcome, you feel helpless.

Helplessness soon becomes hopelessness. When you feel hopeless, you probably aren't going to be motivated to put much energy into trying to make things better, and are likely to give up.

People who deal well with adversity usually approach things very differently. They typically have a strong sense of control over their lives. When you have a sense of control,

- you believe that you have the skills necessary to overcome challenges and adversity.
- you believe that your actions will make a difference in the outcome, and
- you are willing to act on that basis.

A sense of control carries with it the belief that you can cushion and rise above the hurtful impact of a situation by the way you look at it and react to it. It is a refusal to be victimized by people or circumstances.

Let me introduce Joan and Diane. They illustrate this point very well. Joan and Diane are equally smart, talented, and educated. They each want the same thing in life—to be successful. They both have goals and dreams, and they both start their journeys towards fulfillment with similar challenges. Neither of them seems to have a measurable advantage over the other.

Joan is just starting to build a new career. She believes in herself and frequently reminds herself, "I can do this!" She is 100% committed to the vision she has for her life. She remains focused, accomplishes a good deal in a short amount of time, stays organized, and steadily moves toward her goals. Although she faces many difficulties along the way, Joan is resilient, and thinks of these obstacles as challenges rather than catastrophes as she works toward the achievement of her goals.

Diane has a different story. Before she even begins her new career, she has doubts about her ability. She frequently tells herself that she doesn't have enough experience or enough education. She is afraid that she might fail, and believes that if she fails, her whole life will be ruined. When she encounters stress and adversity, she either beats herself up unmercifully, or she blames her circumstances or others for her failures. She can usually provide more reasons why something won't work than ideas for how it can work. Diane plods along, frequently thrown off track by pitfalls and mudslides. After a period of struggling and suffering, Diane will ultimately give up, dejected and feeling like a failure.

You may recognize yourself in Joan or Diane, or perhaps somewhere in between. As you might guess, the chances that each of these people will achieve their goals and create a successful career are dramatically different. Joan has the self-talk, the mindset, and the actions that will keep her on a success path. Joan is a success magnet: She attracts success. Diane, on the other hand, barely gives success a chance. She tells herself that she doesn't have what it takes to be successful—and her actions reflect that belief. Diane is a success deflector. Success bounces right off (and away from) her!

The difference between Joan and Diane is that when problems occur in the form of stress and adversity, Diane doesn't believe that there is anything she can do that will make a difference. She feels inadequate and helpless, is quickly discouraged, and

> *"We can't always choose our circumstances, but we can consciously choose how we are going to respond."*

tends to give up easily. Joan, on the other hand, realizes that she can't necessarily change the circumstances, but she can consciously choose how she is going to respond and find ways of continuously moving toward her goals. The extent to which Joan and Diane are successful in achieving their goals is going to depend, in large part, on the ability of each to respond effectively to adversity.

Our Response To Adversity

Adversity is the most likely obstacle to the achievement of our goals. Think about it. We all live with some level of difficulties in our lives such as job loss, failure to receive a promotion we had hoped for, conflict in an important relationship, or being diagnosed with a serious illness. Every day we see individuals responding to adversity in many different ways, ranging from feelings of helplessness and despair to feelings of empowerment and hope. Whether you feel helpless or empowered is closely related to your sense of control over your life. The importance of having a perception of control over your life has been well documented by researchers. The question becomes, "How do we gain that sense of control?" The answer is, "We consciously learn how to empower ourselves!"

Helplessness vs. Empowerment

There is a continuum between success and failure. Closely related to that continuum is the continuum between empowerment and helplessness. Each of us is somewhere on that continuum. Where you fall on that continuum is going to play a big role in how motivated you are to keep trying even in the

"Where you fall on the continuum between empowerment and helplessness will play a big role in how likely you are to be successful."

33

most difficult circumstances, and how likely you are to succeed. Where you fall on the continuum between empowerment and helplessness will be a major factor in how likely you are to achieve your goals.

EMPOWERMENT

10

9

8

7

6

This line separates those who persevere from those who give up.

RISE ABOVE IT!

5

4

3

2

1

HELPLESSNESS

At the low end of the continuum is *helplessness.* As we have seen, you are likely to feel helpless when you believe that

- you have little control over the situation, and
- nothing you can do will affect the outcome.

People at the low end of the continuum are often in crisis. They frequently feel like victims of their circumstances, and depend on others to solve the problem or make things right.

At the other end of the continuum is *empowerment.* Empowerment comes with the perception that

- your actions will have an impact on the outcome, and
- you have the skills to implement the necessary actions.

In other words, you have a sense of control over your life; you feel empowered.

Like Diane in our example, those who feel helpless frequently get stuck in a mode of blaming themselves excessively or blaming others because they didn't get the results they wanted in their lives. They might say something like, "If I had a different boss, I would

be a lot more successful at my job." Or they might
choose to ignore the problem, telling themselves that
if they just wait long enough, things will get better.
The problem with putting energy into blaming or
ignoring is that we lose our personal power when we
don't take responsibility for getting the results we want.
Can you think of a time when you blamed someone
else or ignored a problem, hoping it would get better?
I sure can! It's painful, isn't it? I remember early in my
marriage, I had no idea what I wanted my own life to
look like. I saw myself as a reflection of my husband
and his career, and gave little thought to what I wanted
my own life to be all about. When I began feeling
dissatisfied and unfulfilled, my first response was to
blame him for not making me happy. I actually believed
that my happiness—or lack of it—was his
responsibility. As a result of that belief, I felt helpless
and victimized by my circumstances. Fortunately, I
soon began to "get it" that my happiness and sense of
fulfillment were up to me. I needed to decide what I
wanted and get rid of my old beliefs about who was
responsible for my life and my happiness.

Those who function toward the empowerment end of the scale are usually very resilient and hold themselves accountable for getting

> *"Those who feel empowered ask, "What can I do about this situation that will improve the outcome."*

the results they want. They consciously take charge of the quality of their own lives, and they develop response-ability by asking, "What can I do about this situation that will improve the outcome?"

The truth is that sometimes we really do have rotten circumstances or situations. What you tell yourself about your ability to deal effectively with these difficult situations affects where you are on this continuum, and how likely you are to keep trying and be successful at achieving your goals.

Take a moment and think of a particular stressful situation that you have experienced. Think about what you told yourself about your ability to affect the outcome. If you essentially told yourself, "I can achieve the outcome I want—I can make this happen," you are at the high end of the empowerment continuum. If you told yourself, "I'm not smart enough, experienced enough"—or words to that effect—you may be experiencing some learned helplessness. As you have probably figured out, people who give up and fail are usually on the helplessness end of the continuum. People who succeed in moving toward their goals and who take responsibility for the quality of their lives are on the empowerment end of the continuum.

If you have ever watched James Bond or Woody Allen movies, you have seen the classic prototypes of empowerment and helplessness. The James Bond character is incredibly cool as he calmly and confidently does whatever super-heroes do. On the other hand, the characters portrayed by Woody Allen usually reflect insecurity and a fixation on how bad things could possibly get. Making a decision about what to have for lunch is enough to cause an ulcer!

LEARNED HELPLESSNESS

In his well-known research experiments in which dogs received mild electrical shocks, Martin Seligman demonstrated that helplessness can, indeed, be learned. Learned helplessness is about the loss of perceived control over adverse events. The dogs in the experiment that had some control over the shock or who could get away took action. Those who had no way of controlling or escaping the shock learned, in effect, that they were helpless. They learned that their actions made no difference. When they realized that they had no control over the situation, they felt powerless and victimized. They had no motivation to continue their efforts, began showing signs of depression, and eventually gave up.

Seligman's work is viewed as landmark research because it provides tremendous insight into why some people keep persevering toward their goals and why others become discouraged and give up. Like the dogs in the experiment, people also learn to be helpless if they have the perception that they have no power over their circumstances. If their actions will make no difference, there is little motivation to keep trying. Learned helplessness is an incredibly destructive mindset that will quickly drain your energy, your persistence, your productivity, and your effectiveness.

Empowerment

The good news is that empowerment can also be learned. Success is about taking control of your life, and consistently moving forward toward the achievement of your goals. The achievement of control comes through the conscious process of empowerment, the *sine qua non* of success. I am defining empowerment as having the mindset and life skills that promote a perception of control, and equip you to be successful in dealing with change and challenges, and the lifestyle that allows you to maintain that success.

> *"Empowerment is having the mindset and the life skills that promote a perception of control, and equip you to be successful in dealing with change and challenges, and the lifestyle that allows you to maintain that success."*

A typical day for someone with a sense of empowerment can be very different from the usual day for someone who has low self-esteem and does not feel empowered. For example, when I feel empowered, I feel optimistic. I don't question my self-worth. My sense of self-efficacy is strong. I know I am capable and effective. I wake up in the morning looking forward to a nice day. I enjoy conversation with my husband while I am dressing, and then I'm off to work. At work I am highly motivated, organized and efficient. I'm able to prioritize my tasks for the day, and complete them with plenty of energy left to enjoy friends and family when I get home. When I don't feel empowered in a particular situation, I tend to be more pessimistic and lower in energy, partly from worrying during the night about yesterday's problems or what might happen tomorrow. I am more irritable and more likely to "nit pick" with my husband. At work, I might have trouble starting projects because I don't feel my usual sense of confidence and competence.

When you take steps toward becoming more empowered, you significantly improve your response to change, and you definitely increase your chances for success. You become empowered when you do what it takes to gain knowledge, skills, and the belief in your own ability to alter the aspects of your life over which you have some control. When you are empowered, you have everything you need to strengthen your ability to overcome difficult challenges and achieve the success and fulfillment you want in your life.

Assessment:

The following statements will help you identify whether you typically function above the line toward Empowerment or below the line toward the Helplessness end of the continuum.

Put a check by any of the following statements that are true for you. These statements are indicators that you might be functioning below the line.

_____1. You aren't clear about what you are trying to achieve.

_____2. You feel that you have no control over your situation.

_____3. You feel victimized by your circumstances.

42

___4. You often feel pessimistic about how thingswill turn out.

___5. You tend to be very hard on yourself when things go wrong.

___6. You tend to blame others when things go wrong.

___7. You think more in terms of why something can't be done, rather than how it could be accomplished.

___8. You are willing to accept much less than the original results you were striving for.

___9. You are likely to ignore problems, hoping that they will go away.

___10. You become discouraged and tend to give up when someone tells you "It can't be done."

If any of the above statements are true for you, (even just sometimes!) this book can help you start moving toward the Empowerment end of the continuum, rise above the adversity that occurs in your life, and achieve the success you desire.

The following characteristics demonstrate resilience, the attitudes that promote empowerment, and the likelihood that you will achieve the results you want. Check any of the following statements that apply to you. They indicate that you are probably functioning above the line.

___1. You quickly recognize and acknowledge adverse situations.

___2. You assess the situation objectively rather than conjuring up all the possible things that could go wrong (catastrophizing.)

___3. You refuse to spend your energy on things you can't control.

___4. You take control by owning the parts of your circumstances that you may have contributed to and take the necessary steps to improve the situation.

___5. You continuously develop life skills that will help you reach your goals.

___6. You welcome challenges.

___7. You are aware when you are functioning below the line, and quickly take steps to empower yourself.

___8. Your typical response to adversity is "How can I rise above it and achieve the results I want."

___9. When things go wrong you pick yourself up and push forward rather than wallowing in disappointment.

___10. You believe in yourself and your ability to handle difficult situations in a constructive way.

Congratulate yourself for each item you checked. These attitudes and behaviors will definitely empower you to rise above difficult circumstances that may occur in your life, and keep you moving toward the results you want.

How Can I Become Empowered?

Becoming empowered requires that you build a strong personal foundation. At the heart of that foundation is:

"At the heart of a strong personal foundation is a mindset that promotes resilience, life skills for effectiveness, and a lifestyle that supports success."

- a mindset that promotes resilience,
- life skills for effectiveness, and
- a lifestyle that supports success.

A mindset that promotes resilience is a mindset of hardiness. In a research study during the breakup of AT&T, researcher Suzanne Oullette conducted a study of executives at Illinois Bell Telephone. She identified three characteristics that clearly differentiate the mindsets

45

of those who thrive and are willing to take on challenges despite adversity from those who fold under pressure. These characteristics are Control, Challenge, and Commitment— the "3 C's of Hardiness"—and will be discussed in detail in Chapter 3. Briefly, however:

- **Control** is the belief that we can influence the outcome of an adverse situation instead of becoming the victim of it.
- **Challenge** means the ability to look at change and/or adversity as an opportunity for growth and improvement rather than believing that change is threatening or catastrophic.
- **Commitment** is an attitude of involvement in what is happening around you—a dedication to yourself, your work, your family, and other important values in your life.

It is highly probable that Joan, our success magnet, ranks very high on the empowerment scale. Diane, our success deflector, probably feels very little control over her life, and would function more toward the helplessness end of the scale. While Diane may feel somewhat committed to her goals, we already know that she is easily thrown off track and tends to get discouraged when she encounters problems, rather than viewing her problems as challenges and persevering.

It is important to deeply understand—"get it in your bones"—that the characteristics of hardiness are essential to motivation, the ability to persevere in difficult times, and to the attainment of success. Even more important is the knowledge that even if these characteristics are not well developed now, *they can be learned.* People can develop certain philosophies of living, a certain mindset that becomes the basis of your self-talk, and certain strategies by which hardiness—resilience to stress and adversity—can be achieved.

It takes time and a strong commitment to change beliefs and old ways of responding and doing things. If you have gained an awareness of where you are on the Empowerment Continuum, you can now begin to identify what you need to do to rise above the line toward Empowerment—and function there on a regular basis. People are better able to make change and become more effective and more successful in their lives when they have a clear path to follow that will lead them to the achievement of their goals. The Model for Success and the five strategies that accompany it provide that path. Good luck on your journey!

IN A NUTSHELL

1. Success is defined as the degree to which one moves forward and upward, progressing in one's lifelong mission, despite all obstacles or other forms of adversity.

2. Adversity is any situation or event that has the potential to discourage you and/or get in the way of achieving your goals.

3. The key to whether you will keep trying and ultimately achieve your goal or get discouraged and give up often lies in how well you manage stress and adversity.

4. When you have a sense of control over your life,
   ✓ you believe that you have the skills necessary to overcome challenges and adversity.

✓ you believe that your actions will make a difference in the outcome, and

✓ you are willing to act on that basis.

5. We can't always choose our circumstances, but we can consciously choose how we are going to respond.

6. Whether you feel helpless or empowered is closely related to your sense of control over your life.

7. Just as there is a continuum between success and failure, there is also a continuum between empowerment and helplessness.

8. Where you fall on that continuum is going to play a big role in how motivated you are to keep trying, even in the most difficult circumstances, and how likely you are to succeed.

9. Those who function toward the Empowerment end of the scale are usually resilient and hold themselves accountable for getting the results they want.

10. What you tell yourself about your ability to deal effectively with these difficult situations affects where you are on the Empowerment Continuum,

and how likely you are to keep trying and be successful at achieving your goals.

11. Learned helplessness is about the loss of perceived control over adverse events.

12. When you feel you have no control over a situation, you feel powerless, have little motivation, and often eventually give up.

13. Learned helplessness is an incredibly destructive mindset that will quickly drain your energy, your persistence, your productivity, and your effectiveness.

14. The good news is that empowerment can belearned.

15. Success is about taking control of your life and consistently moving forward toward the achievement of your goals.

16. The achievement of control comes through the conscious process of empowering yourself with the mindset and the life skills that promote a perception of control, and equip you to be

successful. A Lifestyle of Self-Care allows you to maintain that success.

17. When you take steps toward becoming more empowered, you significantly improve your response to change, and you definitely increase your chances for success.

● ●

Success Mindset 3
A Mindset of Hardiness

"The greats often became great because they continued to believe in themselves despite apparent failures."
—Michael Gelb & Tony Buzan

The Success Mindset

Can you guess who has the greatest influence over whether or not you are successful in achieving your goals? You're right - - it is YOU and what you tell yourself about your ability to be successful. Whether your goal is to be CEO of your company or simply to enjoy life to the fullest, it is your mindset—the state of mind with which you approach each day's challenges—that will determine the quality of your life, and the degree of success you are likely to experience.

Understanding the importance of your mindset, and what you tell yourself about things that happen in your life, is so incredibly important, and yet, often so elusive. Many famous quotations, such as "As a man thinketh, so shall he be," make reference to the significance of your mindset. Yet, most of us go through our lives without ever questioning or challenging how we think about things and what we tell ourselves about the circumstances of our lives.

While I was teaching stress management workshops for a hospital, I wrote a training manual called, *How to Have a Really Good Life—and Reduce Stress While You're at It.* What a "really good life" means to me is that you're resilient, you're successful in reaching most of your goals, and you live in a state of mental, physical, and spiritual well-being. The starting point for having a really good life is taking responsibility for your mindset.

Your mindset carries with it a tremendous amount of power over your life. It is the frame of reference that shapes what you tell yourself (your self-talk) about whether you are capable of dealing with tough situations, and ultimately, whether you will be successful.

The two concepts have been the most helpful for me in understanding the importance of mindset are:

- It is not what happens to you in life, but how you respond that matters.

- Your mindset and the self-talk generated by your mindset determine how you respond—whether you have the tenacity to rise to the challenges in

"Your mindset is the frame of reference that shapes your belief about whether you are capable of dealing with tough situations."

your life and keep striving toward your goals, or whether you give up.

A few years ago, I was hired by a hospital to participate on a team whose task was to initiate a behavioral health program. The program team was made up of a psychiatrist, a therapist, and a receptionist. We called the program Wellness Link. In a small town where people were very self-conscious about mental health services, it was difficult to attract enough clients to justify the cost of the program. We operated at a financial loss to the hospital for quite some time. Month after month we faced the discouraging challenge of trying to make the program successful. Fortunately, each member on our team and the CEO of the hospital maintained a mindset of hope, optimism, and strong commitment to the program. We focused not on the discouraging financial situation, but on the challenge of finding ways to make the program work. The goals of making the program a success and providing the community with much-needed services gave each team member the strong sense of meaning and purpose we needed to spur us on. Rather than "throw in the towel" when we were discouraged, we remained resilient. We had the mindset of hardiness that allowed us to rise above our discouraging situation and find a way to help the program thrive. I am delighted to say that five years later, the program is alive and healthy, with many community members taking advantage of the services whenever the need arises.

THE MAKEUP OF YOUR MINDSET

One of the exciting things about the research of Martin Seligman, Suzanne Oullette, and others is that they have provided proof that people can learn to create a Mindset of Hardiness. We do this by consciously adopting the beliefs and characteristics of those who deal well with adversity

> "We can learn to create a *Mindset of Hardiness* by adopting beliefs and characteristics of stress-hardy people."

and experience success on a regular basis.

For most of us, our mindset—our outlook on things that happen to us—has been constructed largely from our past experiences. Our mindset may include negative and pessimistic thoughts and beliefs from our past. These limiting beliefs can tend to be very discouraging. Most of us have a little voice in our heads which is sometimes called Your *Critic*. Your *Critic* heavily influences your belief in yourself by pointing out all of your shortcomings and deficiencies. The *Critic* constantly reminds you of all the reasons that you cannot possibly achieve your dreams. *Some of the things your critic might say are:*

- "You are in over your head. You might as well give up."
- "What's wrong with you? You can't do anything right!"

- "You don't have what it takes to be a success with this company."
- "You'd better not lose this job. You'd never get another job."
- "You should be further along than you are on this project. You're going to blow it."
- "That is a totally unrealistic goal. You had better lower your expectations."
- "You can't do that. Everyone will think you're a loser."
- "You better not try, you'll embarrass yourself."

A negative mindset is a very real roadblock to success. In order to overcome negative messages from the past and nurture the encouraging self-talk that accompanies a Mindset of Hardiness, you must carefully and consciously choose to detect and override the aspects of your mindset that generates the *Critic's* negative and limiting comments. Instead, you want to develop a mindset that generates constructive and encouraging self-talk. I love it when my self-talk says, "You go, girl. You can make this happen!" Remember, it is your mindset that shapes the content of your self-talk, and your self-talk is the key to whether or not you believe that you have what it takes to be successful. Like Diane in our earlier

58

example, if you don't believe in your ability to be successful, you will likely give up long before you have achieved your goals. For that reason, it is critically important that you carefully choose the makeup of your personal mindset.

I n my stress management workbook, *How to Have a Really Good Life—and Reduce Stress While You're at It,* I explain the makeup of your mindset by using the analogy of creating a recipe for a cake. In order to bake a really good cake, you have to carefully select the ingredients that have been proven to result in a wonderful cake. You also have to exclude ingredients that you know take away from the quality of the cake. The same principle holds true for creating your mindset. Certain ingredients that you might include in your recipe for your mindset have been proven to contribute to resilience and to the ability to create a successful, healthy and deeply satisfying life. Researchers such as Oullette and Seligman would probably share my belief that the following ingredients must be included in your recipe for your personal Mindset of Hardiness. Each of these is described in more detail below:

- a sense of self-efficacy or personal effectiveness
- an optimistic explanatory style
- the 3 C's of Hardiness: Control, Challenge, and Commitment
- a sense of meaning and purpose
- a clear vision of the life you want

Other ingredients might weaken resilience and detract from success and happiness. Some of those ingredients are:

- a low level of self-confidence
- a pessimistic explanatory style
- anger, resentment, and/or judgmental attitudes toward others
- blame of others and/or unhealthy blame of self when things don't go well

The key is to figure out which ingredients you want to include in your personal mindset and which you want to leave out. It is up to each of us to take responsibility for consciously creating a mindset that takes us away from negative, destructive thinking and self-talk, and moves us toward a more optimistic, constructive approach to our life situations. When you take charge of the mindset with which you approach your life, you are empowering yourself to be successful, happy, and fulfilled, even in the most difficult of times.

Let's talk more about

"By taking charge of your mindset, you empower yourself to be successful, happy, and fulfilled, even in times of adversity."

the "ingredients" of a Mindset of Hardiness.

SELF-EFFICACY: (Personal Effectiveness)

Researcher Albert Bandura has suggested that our ability to succeed in life is closely tied to self-efficacy. Self-efficacy has to do with whether or not we believe ourselves to be effective in dealing with the world and achieving success in our lives.

"Our ability to succeed in life is closely tied to our beliefs about our own personal effectiveness."

Bandura contends that self-efficacy is linked to having a sense of control over situations in our lives, and suggests that two things are essential to a sense of control:

1. The perception that you have the skills to cope with a particular situation, and

61

2. The perception of being able to deal with intrusive negative thoughts that make you feel less competent.

It is clear that we are more likely to be successful if we develop a mindset and self-talk that encourages self-efficacy. When you believe yourself to be effective, you are confident that you have the ability to mobilize the motivation, the cognitive resources, and the courses of action needed to exercise control over events in your life. In other words, you know you have what it takes to rise above adversity and get the job done successfully.

AN OPTIMISTIC EXPLANATORY STYLE

We all have a way of talking to ourselves about things that happen in our lives. What we tell ourselves about the world and our ability to be successful is called our explanatory style. Your explanatory style determines whether your self-talk is positive and encouraging or negative and discouraging Whether your self-talk is constructive or destructive is strongly influenced by whether you have optimistic beliefs or pessimistic beliefs about the world, about others, and about your own ability to be successful. (By the way, the Critic in your head is a pessimist!) People who have adopted a pessimistic attitude toward life feel very little sense of control over their lives. As we know from Chapter One, when people believe that they have no control over their lives, they often develop feelings of helplessness and give up.

Optimism is defined in the dictionary as 1) the tendency to take the most cheerful view of matters or to expect the best outcome, and 2) the practice of looking on the bright side of things. Pessimism is defined as 1) the tendency to expect misfortune, or the worst outcome in any circumstances, and 2) the practice of looking on the dark side of things. Whether you live your life from

> *"Optimism is the practice of looking on the bright side of things and expecting the best outcome. Pessimism is defined as 1) the tendency to expect misfortune, or the worst outcome in any circumstances, and 2) the practice of looking on the dark side of things."*

optimistic beliefs or pessimistic beliefs is a key

determinant in how well
you cope with stress
and adversity, and
whether you are
successful in making
your dreams a reality.
Why? Because beliefs
create actions, and

> *"Whether you live from a mindset of optimism or pessimism is a key determinant in your ability to cope with adversity and achieve success."*

actions determine results.

When adversity occurs in the life of pessimists, they typically assign three personal reasons as causing the problem:

- **Internal:** They blame themselves. A typical response would be "It's all my fault."
- **Global:** They believe that the one incident extends into all parts of their lives. The response would be something like "I mess up everything I do."
- **Stable:** They assume things will never change. The typical response is "It's the story of my life. Things will never change."

Pessimists often believe that when bad things happen in their lives, it is a result of personal failings that are unalterable. If a college student who is pessimistic scored poorly on an exam, she might be likely to say, "I'm too dumb to make good grades in this class. I'll never be able to get it right." Optimists, on the other hand, respond more constructively to adversity by formulating a plan to improve the situation and/or ask others for help. They ask 'What can I do to make the situation better?" and then follow through and do it.

Consider our example of Joan and Diane. Diane is a pessimist. If she were in a work situation where an important staff meeting didn't go well, Diane would probably feel like a failure and assume the meeting went poorly due to her personal shortcomings. Her self-talk would go something like this: "It's all my fault. I'm a bad leader. I seem to screw up everything I do." Even if Diane did not perform well in this one meeting, she will severely dis-empower herself if she writes herself off as a bad leader. She will spend

65

important time and energy thinking about how incompetent she is. This is a very incapacitating approach that will probably make a difficult situation worse.

Joan, who has a more optimistic outlook on life, would approach the same situation something like this: "O.K. I really blew it today, but I'm never going to let that happen again. The next time, I will have prepared myself much more thoroughly and be able to make a dynamite presentation." Joan's time and energy will be used much more constructively.

My all-time favorite mentor, author, and lecturer Joan Borysenko tells a story in her book *Inner Peace for Busy People* that illustrates the difference between optimistic and pessimistic explanatory styles in times of adversity. Joan and her husband had recently bought a new boat. She decided to take the children out on the boat, even though she knew very little about boating. She kept noticing red and green barrels in the water, but had no idea what purpose the barrels served. (The barrels marked which areas of the water were navigable and which were not.) Since she didn't know which areas she should avoid, they eventually ran aground. She was extremely frightened and upset, and her self-talk went something like this:

"It will be a very long time before the tide will be high enough to float free. It is getting colder and we might freeze. I'm such a careless mother to take the boat out with so little knowledge about the barrels. Only a bad mother would do that. On top of this, I have missed several of the PTA meetings. Working mothers should be shot. It's all my fault. I'm a worthless person."

In contrast, she noticed that her 14-year-old son, Justin, was looking very puffed up and happy. When she asked him why he was so happy, he said, "This is the best thing that ever happened to me. I will save us"—and he did! He had everyone get out of the boat, hauled the boat back into deeper water, and soon they were on their way.

What a great story contrasting optimism and pessimism! The mother's self-talk is a classic example of helplessness and pessimism. The self-talk of the son reflected optimism and hope.

While it is important to recognize the reality of your adverse situation, you are far more likely to overcome difficulties in your life and achieve success if you consciously adopt a more constructive, optimistic attitude in the face of adversity. This kind of approach will give you the motivation and the courage to keep striving toward your goals, even in the most difficult of times.

THE 3 C's OF HARDINESS: Control, Challenge, and Commitment

Optimistic people are also stress-hardy people—people who cope well with stress. Researcher Suzanne Oullette identified three attitudes that she says are characteristic of optimistic, stress-hardy people. In Chapter Two, we discussed these characteristics as being essential to empowerment:

- **Control:** Optimistic, stress-hardy people realize that while we can't always control our circumstances, we *can* control our attitudes about our circumstances and how we respond.

68

We can choose to be helpless, complaining victims, or to be proactive creators of our life experiences.

- **Challenge:** Stress-hardy people view adversity as a challenge rather than a catastrophe.

- **Commitment:** Stress-hardy people feel a sense of meaning and purpose in life and a strong commitment to what they value. They choose to be involved with life and with other people, rather than to isolate themselves.

These characteristics are also crucial components of a Mindset of Hardiness. They build the resilience that keeps you moving toward your goals despite the obstacles life may throw in your path. You greatly strengthen your ability to cope with adversity when the 3 C's become integral parts of your mindset.

> *"A sense of control, challenge, and commitment are crucial components of a Mindset of Hardiness."*

The story of Dr. Victor Frankl, a Viennese psychiatrist and author of the book, *Man's Search for Meaning,* provides a great example of control, challenge, and commitment. During his time as a prisoner in Auschwitz and other concentration camps during World War II, Dr. Frankl experienced a profound insight when he realized that his Nazi captors could control his environment, and do whatever they wanted to do with his body, but only he could control his mind. He realized that he had the power to decide within himself how this experience was going to affect him. He took *control* of his state of mind,

> *"He had the power to decide how this experience was going to affect him"*

his mindset, and, in doing so, took control of his situation. He was able to view his horrible situation as a *challenge* not only to survive, but to teach others how one can overcome even the most horrendous circumstances. He made a *commitment* in his own mind to survive and to help others by teaching university students the lessons he learned as a prisoner. With a mindset of control, challenge, and commitment, and the self-talk generated by that mindset, Dr. Frankl was able to transcend his horrible experience of imprisonment and survive when others around him were dying—physically, emotionally, and spiritually. Dr. Frankl's story certainly makes the point that "It is not what happens to you, but how you respond that is important." After his release, Dr. Frankl went on to become a noted author, lecturer, and teacher— definitely an incredible success story. Another illustration of control, challenge, and commitment occurred in the life of my friend and partner, Abby Donnelly, several years ago. Here is Abby's story in her own words:

"I was overwhelmed by the stress of my job. There was constant daily pressure to fix quality problems that occurred at our supplier's plant because, when the supplier quality was poor, our plant could not produce good quality product either. I could not control the supplier operations, but I recognized how important it was to help them improve their systems. For the first few months, every time one of my co-workers complained to me, I became defensive and attacked back. The result was that I lost credibility and support. Then, one day, I realized that I had a choice. I could not change my lack of control over the supplier operations, but I could control how I responded to my co-workers and the supplier. I stopped playing the victim and started asking more questions about the problems they were having. I started rallying the troops to view this as a challenge! I decided that I was going to commit to seeking out resources that could help me solve the problem, accept responsibility as the liaison to the supplier, and make something happen. While the changes did not occur overnight, over the next few months I successfully worked with the supplier to improve the product quality. I also re-established productive, credible relationships with my co-workers."

You May Be A Pessimist If - - - -

Take a moment to think about a bad event that happened to you. What did you tell yourself about why the event happened? If you told yourself that the bad event happened because you are a rotten, worthless person, and you see the event as a fearful, terrible experience, you may be a pessimist. You might feel like a victim, and may get stuck in a sense of helplessness and despair. You may even experience feelings of anger, depression, and hopelessness. On the other hand, if you look back on bad events and notice that you told yourself that they were challenges, and used those events as opportunities for personal growth, you are probably an optimistic and stress-hardy person who embraces change with courage and confidence.

It is crucial to become aware of our own negative attitudes and beliefs that promote the stress response and lead to discouragement, feelings of helplessness, and even physical illness. In so doing, we create the opportunity to adopt the new, more positive beliefs and attitudes that characterize a Mindset of Hardiness. With a Mindset of Hardiness, we can begin to develop the sense of control we need to withstand a tremendous amount of adversity and continually move toward our goals.

A SENSE OF MEANING AND PURPOSE

One of the things that I have become very clear about during my career as a success coach is that the attainment of success and fulfillment in life requires that you know what you are trying to accomplish and why. It requires that you have a clear vision of life as you want it to be and a sense of meaning and purpose in your life. Without a clear vision, you won't know where you are going. If you don't know where you are going, how are you going to get there? Without a

> *The attainment of success and fulfillment in life requires that you know what you are trying to accomplish and why.*

sense of meaning and purpose in your vision, life may not seem very fulfilling. One of the profound things that Dr. Frankl taught as a result of his experience in the Nazi prison camps is that "suffering without meaning equals despair." Frankl writes that those who did not have a sense of meaning and purpose were more likely to give up hope. Those who gave up hope became more vulnerable to the ravages of the diseases that swept through the prison camp. Many quickly died. A sense of meaning and purpose provides us the energy to get through our lives. As Dr. Frankl demonstrated, when we create meaning in our lives by committing to a higher cause or higher vision of ourselves, we are able to get through even the most terrifying and awful of circumstances.

A sense of meaning and purpose in your life enhances commitment to your goals. When you are committed, you are more likely to remain hopeful and keep persevering, even in the most difficult of times. As we know, it is those who persevere that reach the top. Those who give up or stop short of their goals often settle for far less than their original dream.

When I began my work with Wellness Link, the hospital's behavioral health program, I wasn't quite sure I had the skills or experience that the job required. One thing I *was* sure of, however, was that the creation of a behavioral health center where the residents of our town and surrounding towns could receive help for emotional problems was a part of my life purpose. My passion for the creation of that program quickly overcame any doubts or fears I might have had. As a result, I was able to focus fully on what would make that program work, and not the reasons why it wouldn't work. My dedication and sense of purpose was all the motivation I needed to keep plugging away, even when things seemed incredibly bleak.

A CLEAR VISION

Your sense of meaning and purpose shape your vision—your dream for your life. It is your vision for life as it can be that motivates you. Passionately wanting to make your vision a reality gives you the hope you need in order to see the negative events in your life as simply a challenge that can be overcome rather than something catastrophic. A vision serves as a compass. It gives you a sense of direction and the impetus for action. It keeps you focused on what you really want in life and the steps you need to take to get there. It is your vision that provides you with a compelling reason to persevere. Without a clear idea about what you want your future to look like, it is easy to become discouraged and even give up when life throws challenges in your path.

> *"It is your vision for life as it can be that motivates you and serves as your compass."*

It is helpful if your vision for your life is based on your definition of success. In order to have a clear vision for your life, it is important for you to know what success means for you. Does success mean making a six-figure income or a million dollars in the bank, or does it mean a particular job title? Does success mean feeling happy and fulfilled on a daily basis? How are you going to know when you are successful? So often, as I am talking with my coaching clients, I discover that they have no sense of direction. They have no clear vision for the future, no definition of success or fulfillment, and have not given much thought to what gives them a sense of meaning and purpose.

Your vision for success doesn't have to be about a career choice. It can be a vision of the kind of person you want to be, the environment in which you wish to live, and the kind of people you wish to surround yourself with. The vision for your life can be something as simple as deciding whether you want to live your life as a stressed out over-achiever, or as a person who enjoys balancing career, fun, family, and friends. I used to think that in order to be successful, I had to be a very serious, hard-driving, achievement-oriented person. That was my vision of a successful person. I thought that if I ever "let up," I might become a lazy couch potato who wouldn't have a chance at a successful career. It never occurred to me that having fun and enjoying life are just as important in life as career achievement. Fortunately, my vision of myself has changed over the years. I still want success in my career, but I have learned that I won't become any less productive or less successful by including fun and friends in my vision for my life. In fact, I am more productive because my energy level is higher.

Who Are You and What Do You Want?

Perhaps the concept of having a vision, a sense of meaning and purpose, and knowing what you want is best illustrated in the wonderful story about a philosopher by the name of Peter Russell. As many people do, Peter had an answering machine. If you were to call him, and he was unable to come to the phone, you would hear the following message:

"This is not an answering machine. It is a questioning machine. Who are you and what do you want? In case you think these are frivolous questions, they are not. Most people come into this world, and

78

leave it again without having answered either question."

Who are you, and what do you want? We often believe that external things are what define success, that these things give us our identity and bring us the happiness that we are seeking. In reality, what many people experience when they find that they have the income they wanted—or the big house—or the fancy car—is an initial sense of euphoria and excitement, which is often quickly replaced by a sense of letdown when the excitement wears off. They still don't have the *feeling* they want in their lives. They don't have a sense of fulfillment. Soon they begin seeking something bigger and better. They instinctively know that there is something more to life, but what is it they are missing?

It is my belief that what is missing for many people is the strong sense of meaning and purpose and the clear vision that comes with a Mindset of Hardiness. Take a little time to give some thought to the questions, "Who am I?" and "What do I want?" Your personal reflection on these questions, and a strong commitment to your vision and your sense of meaning and purpose, will help you begin to lock in your Mindset of Hardiness. It is that Mindset of Hardiness that will equip you with the resiliency you need to overcome life's difficulties and achieve the success you want in your life. Perhaps the importance of having a Mindset of Hardiness that includes a clear vision for your life and a strong sense of meaning and purpose, is best described by George Bernard Shaw who said:

"This is the true joy of life: the being used for a purpose, recognized by yourself as a mighty one; the being thoroughly worn out before you are thrown on the scrap heap; the being a force of nature instead of a feverish selfish clod of ailments and grievances complaining that the world will not devote itself to making you happy."

In this vein, I encourage you to create for yourself a mindset that supports a life that is filled with a mighty purpose, lived to the fullest, and immersed in a spirit of joy, gratitude and fulfillment.

IN A NUTSHELL

1. It is your mindset that will determine the quality of your life, and the degree of success that you are likely to experience.

2. Your mindset is the frame of reference that shapes what you tell yourself about whether you are capable of dealing with tough situations.

3. It is not what happens to you in life, but how you respond that matters. Your mindset determines how you respond.

4. Your mindset shapes the content of your self-talk.

5. The ingredients of a mindset of hardiness are:

   - A sense of self-efficacy or personal effectiveness
   - An optimistic explanatory style
   - The 3 C's of Hardiness: Control, Challenge, and Commitment
   - A sense of meaning and purpose
   - A clear vision of the life you want

6. By taking charge of your mindset, you empower yourself to be successful, happy, and fulfilled, even in times of adversity.

7. Self-efficacy is linked to having a sense of control.

8. Essential to a sense of control are:
   ✓ The perception that you have the skills to cope with a particular situation, and
   ✓ The perception of being able to deal with intrusive negative thoughts that make you feel less competent.

9. You are more likely to be successful if you develop the mindset and self-talk that encourages self-efficacy.

10. Whether you live from a mindset of optimism or a mindset of pessmism is a key determinant in how well you cope with adversity and whether you are successful in making your dreams a reality.

11. Optimism is the practice of looking on the bright side of things and expecting the best outcome.

12. Essential components of a Mindset of Hardiness are a sense of control, challenge, and commitment.

13. The attainment of success and fulfillment in life requires that you know what you are trying to accomplish and why. Your vision provides direction; your sense of meaning and purpose provides fulfillment.

• •

Life Skills For Effectiveness 4

In today's fast-paced society, it is a given that most of us are going to have a lot of stress and adversity in our lives. The key is to make sure we have the skills with which to handle such challenges. Life Skills for Effectiveness give us the tools we need to retain a sense of control and empowerment. As we strengthen and develop our life skills, we increase our ability to respond effectively to obstacles and to keep persevering toward our goals.

> *"As we strengthen and develop our life skills, we increase our ability to respond effectively to obstacles and to keep persevering toward our goals."*

The main reason that we become stressed and discouraged in difficult circumstances is that the situation feels beyond our control. In my own life, the primary trigger for stress and feelings of helplessness are situations in which I have the belief that there is nothing I can do to make things better. On the other hand, when I can make responses that I believe will be effective in

"A sense of control plays a key role in the ability to rise above adversity and persevere toward your goals."

achieving the outcome I want, I feel a sense of control, and will keep trying.

There are many life skills that contribute significantly to the strong personal foundation that allows you to maintain a sense of control and resilience. The skills listed below are the ones I have found to be most helpful.

- Eliciting the relaxation response on a regular basis,
- Reframing your perspective on challenging situations,
- Communicating effectively,
- Renewing your energy,
- Managing your time,
- Maintaining a sense of humor,

- Managing your finances, and
- Networking effectively.

ELICITING THE RELAXATION RESPONSE ON A REGULAR BASIS

You may be surprised to find relaxation included in a chapter on "Life Skills for Effectiveness." We don't usually think of relaxation as a skill. In fact, many of us have a nagging little belief that tells us that learning to relax will take away our competitive edge and dull our motivation. In reality, just the opposite is true. Learning to relax deeply is a skill that could save your life. Let me explain.

We know that in today's frenzied world, many of us live with chronic stress and frequent adversity. As a result, we are likely to experience fear, anger, anxiety, depression, and other emotions that usually have negative effects on our sense of well-being. However, how stress affects us physically is of equal importance.

When faced with pressures and worries, we often react to these acute, chronic stressful situations with a physiological response commonly known as the stress response or the "fight-or-flight" response. When this occurs, our bodies are telling us that stress has reached the level of *distress.* The stress response is controlled in an area of the brain called the hypothalamus. When confronted with a perceived threat, the limbic system, which regulates sexual impulse, pain, hunger, fear, and anger, responds to the stress by gathering input from our thoughts and emotions and relaying information to the hypothalamus. The hypothalamus causes the sympathetic nervous system to release chemicals that prepare the body to fight or flee by providing us with increased energy.

When under stress, we may experience the physical symptoms of:

- *increased* blood pressure,
- *increased* heart rate,
- *increased* rate of breathing,
- *increased* tension, and/or
- *increased* metabolism.

The pituitary gland, also receiving stress signals from the limbic system, releases adrenaline and other stress-related hormones, thus adding to our preparation for fight or flight. Your body isn't able to distinguish between the life-threatening situations that faced our ancestors (lions and tigers) and the stressors you experience in your everyday life. In fact, just *thinking* about a stressful situation can trigger the fight-or-flight response!

The following is an example of how the mind/body connection handles new, potentially stressful information:

You are a single, working parent with a five-year-old daughter and a three-year-old son. You receive a telephone call from a staff member of your children's day care center saying that they won't be able to take care of your children tomorrow. You may say to yourself something like this: "Oh, no! What am I going to do with the children? I am scheduled to attend the company strategic planning session with my boss tomorrow. I can't tell my boss that I'm busy elsewhere and stay home. My parents are on vacation, my sister lives in Atlanta, and the person I usually use for a baby sitter is out of town. What am I going to do?"

Your body quickly responds to your fearful thoughts. Your heart races, your blood pressure increases, your breath becomes shallow, and your stomach is rolling around. You are experiencing a typical fight-or-flight response.

If you are living a life filled with chronic stress, your body is continually reacting with the fight-or-flight response. Sooner or later, you are likely to begin to see some negative physiological signs and symptoms of stress, such as high blood pressure, ulcers, heart attacks, strokes, lowered immune ability, back pain, sleep disturbance, and indigestion. You may experience other symptoms, such as fear, anxiety, depression, anger, irritability, trouble thinking clearly, constant worry, forgetfulness, inability to make decisions, loss of sense of humor, loss of your "sense of direction" in life, compulsive eating, over-medicating, excessive use of alcohol or other drugs—the list goes on and on.

Chronic stress also affects our productivity. In the late 1970's, Herbert Benson, M.D., Associate Professor of Medicine at the Mind/Body Medical Institute of Harvard Medical School, wrote an article for the *Harvard Business Review* describing the relationship between stress and productivity. This relationship is known as the Yerkes-Dodson Law. Interestingly, as stress increases, so does productivity—to a point. When stress becomes chronic or excessive in terms of amount or duration, things start to go downhill, and productivity decreases. In a nutshell, mild to moderate stress can motivate you, and result in increased productivity. More serious or chronic stress leads to poor productivity.

I recently experienced a perfect example of the Yerkes-Dodson Law in my own life. My husband and I had invited guests for dinner. The guests were to arrive at 6:00 P.M. In my mind, I knew exactly what cleaning still needed to be done, and what I needed to do to prepare the dinner. I experienced some mild stress since I don't entertain all that often, and I wasn't quite sure how long all the tasks on my "to do" list would take. The stress was serving as a motivator, however, and I was pretty much on top of things. The thing that caused me to shift from a healthy stress level to unhealthy distress was that, as I planned my time, I had forgotten to include a business conference call which I had scheduled. The call was to last an hour-and-a-half. Suddenly, I had serious doubts about whether I could get everything accomplished before the guests arrived, and the stress level increased dramatically. I began to feel frustrated, lost my focus, and felt overwhelmed by the amount of work remaining to be done and the shortage of time. I was definitely on "overload" and almost became immobilized from the anxiety. My productivity diminished because I was having trouble maintaining my focus. I had the sudden realization that this is what the Yerkes-Dodson Law is all about!" I did get all my tasks accomplished, but I felt mentally and physically exhausted.

Most people who are highly productive do a balancing act. They function on the high end of the stress range, pushing the upper limits in terms of stress and productivity, and they are close to burnout. Learning to relax would shift them back toward the top of the U curve. Their productivity would be greater, and the stress damage to their body would be less.

Because of the harmful effects of chronic stress on your health and on your ability to be productive and effective, it is essential to recognize when you are experiencing symptoms of stress, and to find ways to control and neutralize these effects. Developing a regular practice of eliciting the relaxation response—your body's built-in mechanism for reversing the physiological effects of the fight-or-flight response—is a good place to start. Most stress-hardy people try to relax for at least fifteen minutes a day. Consciously relaxing your mind and body on a regular basis gives your body the opportunity for healing and renewal.

The relaxation response is the opposite of the fight-or-flight response. It causes a physiological response that brings about a reduction in sympathetic nervous system activity. Just as stimulating the hypothalamus causes the stress response to occur, reducing the stimulation results in relaxation. When the relaxation response is elicited, we experience:

- *decreased* blood pressure,
- *decreased* heart rate,
- *decreased* breathing rate,
- *decreased* muscle tension, and
- *decreased* metabolism.

While the fight-or-flight response usually occurs automatically (that is, involuntarily), and sometimes even without our awareness, we have to consciously bring about the relaxation response. Dr. Benson was one of the first people to point out the importance of the relaxation response. He developed a technique called *"Respiratory One"* by which we can consciously elicit the relaxation response. This technique helps us slow down and helps defuse the body's responses to anxiety, fear, worry and other stress-producing emotions. Dr. Benson's technique and others will be discussed in the strategies presented in Section Two. While I have chosen to list the relaxation response with life skills, eliciting the relaxation response on a regular basis is also an important part of a lifestyle of self-care, which we will discuss in the next chapter.

REFRAMING YOUR PERSPECTIVE ON CHALLENGING SITUATIONS

Many of the strategies for increasing personal effectiveness and achieving success are designed around building a greater sense of personal control. One of the most effective ways of increasing your sense of personal control is reframing your perspective. Among therapists, this process is known as *cognitive restructuring*. Reframing

> "Reframing your perspective on challenging situations can help promote a sense of control."

or cognitive restructuring are just fancy ways of saying that you consciously change the way you are perceiving a situation. You redesign your perceptions about things that happen to you. The technique of cognitive restructuring is frequently used in the field of cognitive therapy. One of the main concepts in cognitive therapy is this: It isn't a particular situation or even other people that determine whether we become stressed,

95

> *"Our perception of a situation is the major cause of how we respond emotionally, behaviorally, and physiologically."*

frightened, upset, or angry. It is our perception of the situation that is the major cause of how we respond emotionally, behaviorally, and physiologically. In other words, what you tell yourself about things determines how you experience them.

Here's an example: You find yourself in a traffic jam that has you at a standstill. If it is 7:45 A.M., and you are on your way to work with a meeting to make at 8 o'clock, you might react by thinking, "Oh no! I'm going to be late! This is the story of my life. Whatever can go wrong, does! My boss will be furious. I may even get fired." Your body is tense, your blood pressure rises, and you notice the beginnings of a throbbing headache. However, if the traffic jam occurs on a weekend, you may find that your reaction is quite different, and that you aren't bothered in the least. You may think to yourself, "Oh well, since there is nothing I can do about it, I might as well relax and enjoy the new CD I just bought." In both cases, the event was the same. You were in a traffic jam. But your reactions were different. Your reaction depended on the meaning you assigned to the traffic jam—your self-talk about the traffic jam. It is empowering to know that while you may not be able to change your situation, you have the choice to empower yourself by changing your frame of reference.

E ach of us spends a tremendous amount of time engaged in self-talk—describing and interpreting life events to ourselves. To the extent that your self-talk reflects reality, you will be able to think clearly, remain calm, and make wise decisions. When your self-talk is based on an exaggerated, sometimes distorted perception of reality, you are likely to experience feelings of anger, fear,

> *"Even though you may not be able to change your situation, you can change your frame of reference about the situation."*

sadness, and/or inadequacy. You are also likely to experience stress. Here is an example:

Sam decides to end a long-standing relationship with Jennifer. Jennifer's self-talk may be, "I can't live without Sam." That is a great example of self-talk prompted by an irrational belief. Physically healthy people don't die merely from being alone. You may prefer not to be alone and it may cause you to feel sad, but most people can and do live through it.

Reframing is about identifying your self-talk in various situations, examining and challenging the self-talk and old beliefs that are no longer serving you well, testing your self-talk to determine whether your thinking is constructive or destructive, and restructuring your negative, discouraging self-talk to be more optimistic and beneficial.

Negative, destructive responses to stress and adversity are often habitual. In other words, those responses have become automatic over time. You don't stop to think or choose, and you end up feeling victimized. Again, the key to cognitive restructuring lies in the recognition that our feelings and behavioral responses aren't caused by the situation, but by how we think about a situation. Have you ever noticed that how you think about an event creates your reality? If Jennifer tells herself that she can't live without Sam, that belief will become her reality. Your thoughts and self-talk are like personal myths. You may believe them without even being aware of them, and almost always without appraising them realistically.

When you blame your situation or another person for your feeling or your actions ("My boss makes me feel so inadequate. No wonder I screw up all the time."), you are giving up your sense of control and becoming a victim. It is helpful to look at your situation from another perspective and put your thoughts and self-talk in a more constructive mode. For example, "My boss is definitely a challenge, but I have what it takes to do this job well" is a wiser, more creative, and more productive response. And, best of all, when you consciously restructure your response, you regain your sense of control, which is essential for effective functioning.

Reframing is not about denying that there are times when it is appropriate to feel anxious, angry, frustrated, or even depressed. These emotions are often necessary to motivate you to overcome barriers and make needed changes to achieve your goals. What is important is the understanding that our perceptions and self-talk influence our feelings. The goal is to avoid or at least challenge thoughts and self-talk that are destructive and disempowering. Every day we have a choice about the frame of reference from which we will view our various situations. Is a traffic jam going to ruin our day, or are we going to relax and listen to a nice CD? Are the golden hairs that I have to constantly vacuum from the carpet a reason to complain, or just a part of having a beautiful Golden Retriever that loves me dearly? When we learn the

> *"Every day we have a choice about the frame of reference from which we will view our various situations."*

skill of identifying and challenging negative, destructive thoughts and self-talk, and reframing them in a more constructive light, we are in a much stronger position to remain resilient and persevere toward our goals. Strategies for learning to recognize and restructure dis-empowering perceptions and self-talk will be found in Section II.

COMMUNICATING EFFECTIVELY

All relationships, whether business relationships or intimate ones, grow stronger and happier when we care about and pay attention to the way we communicate. Effective communication can contribute greatly to how you handle adversity. It can help you avoid stressful situations and resolve difficult situations that have already occurred in your life.

Communication has many components. The verbal component is what you say and how you say it. Listening, hearing, and understanding comprise the listening component. A third component is your non-verbal communication which includes your body language, eye contact, and your actions. Have you ever had someone say to you, "I can tell just by looking at you that you're upset?" I certainly have! Actions really do speak louder than words!

You can greatly increase your sense of personal control and effectiveness by examining the way you communicate. Examples of effective communication include being able to express your likes and dislikes, knowing how to accept a compliment, and knowing when to say "yes" and when to say "no"—and mean it!

The way other people respond to you is almost always affected by how you communicate. The communication of people who are truly effective is usually open, honest, and appropriate, typically enhancing self-esteem and nurturing relationships. The communication of less effective people often tends to be in a style of blaming, denying, and attacking. Needless to say, that style of communication is damaging to self-esteem and to relationships. It also tends to contribute to a high level of stress in your life.

Communication Styles

The style we use to communicate with others often determines how effective we are in both our business and personal relationships. The following are examples of some communication styles:

- Assertive Communication: This style of communicating gives the message, "I am important and you are important.."
- Aggressive Communication: This form of communication gives the message, "I am important, but you aren't."
- Passive-Aggressive Communication: I consider this an underhanded way of communicating. It gives the message, "I am important and you aren't important, but I'm not going to tell you that."
- Passive Communication: This is the communication of the victim. It gives the message, "You're the one that is important. I am not important."

It won't come as a surprise to you that the most effective of these communication styles is assertive. Assertive communication is powerful because you speak and act from awareness and choice. You are aware of your alternatives, and you choose to communicate from a place of calmness, with a focus on the resolution of the problem. This type of communication not only enhances relationships, but also self-esteem. You are expressing yourself and getting your needs met. Self-expression, when it is open, honest, and appropriate, usually feels good to you and to the other person as well. When you communicate effectively, you express your likes and dislikes, accept a compliment, and know when to say "yes" and when to say "no." When you communicate effectively, you say how you feel when it is appropriate, and ask for what you need. Aggressive communication is attacking and destructive, often stemming from negative, automatic reactions.

Three keys, then, to effective communication are:
1. You act out of awareness and choice.
2. You express your feelings openly, honestly, and appropriately.
3. You encourage the other person to express his or her feelings.

It is easy to become so emotionally hooked in a situation that you don't share your feelings openly, or you don't really hear what the other person is trying to communicate to you. Training in self-assertion contributes greatly to a personal sense of control by helping you become more aware of your own needs and values and learning to express them with honesty and kindness.

RENEWING YOUR ENERGY

In a fast-paced world of endless "to do" lists, we expend huge amounts of energy. If we don't take time to renew our energy, we will quickly burn out. It is essential to take charge of your life, and make time for energy renewal.

Three ways to set the stage for energy renewal are:
- learning to say no,
- setting boundaries, and
- getting rid of energy drains.

Here is an energy analogy that works well for me. Picture in your mind a beautiful golden cup. Now, imagine that the cup contains your life energy. Each time someone asks you to do something, you reach into that cup and take out some of the energy. As people ask you to do more and more, you keep

> *"It is essential to take charge of your life, and make time for energy renewal."*

reaching into the cup for energy. Can you imagine what happens to that cup if you are constantly giving out energy, but never replenishing it? Suddenly, the cup is empty. You are exhausted, stressed out, and burnt out. There is nothing more to give.

Your golden cup must be refilled on a regular basis. You refill your cup by learning to nurture yourself and becoming a good steward of your life energy. You consciously decide how your energy will be used, and you make sure your cup gets refilled.

Learn To Say No

One way to avoid draining your cup is to learn to say "no" to things that are less important to you. Regardless of how busy or overwhelmed we are, many of us have a hard time saying "no" when we are asked by our friends, family members, colleagues, or customers to take on "just one more thing." Women, in particular, get caught up in wanting to please, and in feeling guilty if they say "no."

Have you ever had the experience of feeling like you need to say "no" in a situation, but feared that you would be thought of as selfish if you did? I have struggled with that one most of my adult life. Fortunately, during my careers as therapist and coach, I have often worked with people who needed to develop that very skill— the art of saying "no". In our practice sessions, I would make requests of my clients, and their goal was to say no to each of the requests, gradually increasing their comfort level while saying no. As we practiced our role plays, I also benefited by improving my own skill at saying "no."

We often get caught up in thinking that we have to justify saying "no." What we don't think about is the toll that trying to please everyone else takes on our energy and health. In fact, if we don't learn to say "no", we could find ourselves well on our way to launching a successful career as a doormat—not the kind of career that most of us had in mind.

Tell the Truth When Saying No

I have found that it is very important to tell the truth when I decide to say "no". If you stick with the truth, you avoid embarrassing situations, and you feel good about yourself. When you say "no", it is usually a good idea not to "over-explain" or try to justify why you are saying "no". I find that the more I try to explain why I'm saying "no", the more people will argue with me. Taking care of yourself is a valid reason for saying "no" that needs little explanation.

Remember, energy is a key ingredient to success. Decide which people and which projects will get your energy by asking yourself, "Does saying 'yes' to this contribute to my sense of meaning and purpose? Does saying 'yes' reflect what I value? Is this related to my high priority goals?" Then say "no" to the rest. And by the way, regardless of which approach you use to say "no," your assertive communication skills will come in handy.

Set Boundaries

You can also use your assertive communication skills to set boundaries. Boundaries are your rules for what other people may and may not say or do to you. Setting appropriate boundaries for other people's behavior is a "must" for maintaining a sense of control over your life. I like the idea that suggests that a boundary is like an emotional immune system. Your physical immune system protects you from invaders such as bacteria, viruses, and parasites. Your emotional immune system protects you from invasions from the words and behaviors of others.

For example, you may have some people in your life who are physically or verbally harmful. You may have others who constantly blame you, put you down, or reprimand you. Someone else may make fun of you in front of others, or discount you or challenge everything you do. It is essential that you assertively let these people know that it's not okay to treat you that way. For example, you might say, "When you yell at me, I feel de-valued and unloved. I need you to talk to me in a calm way that allows us to work constructively toward a solution for this problem." When people refuse to respond to your boundaries and your requests, you may choose to detach and end an unhealthy relationship.

In the strategies section, you will find exercises that help you learn to say no and set boundaries in an assertive, appropriate way.

Getting Rid of Energy Drains

All of us have many things that drain our energy. Sometimes we aren't even consciously aware of our energy drains. Some of the things that most noticeably drain our energy are:

- unmet emotional needs,
- unhealthy eating habits
- unpaid bills,
- lack of financial reserves,
- unhealthy relationships,
- lack of exercise, and
- work you don't enjoy.

Refilling Your Cup

In the chapter on Lifestyle of Self-care, you will learn to replenish your energy on a consistent basis as you begin building conscious relaxation into your schedule, as well as maintaining a healthy diet, exercising on a regular basis, developing a support system, and connecting with your own spirituality. Other things that help refill your cup are:

- spending time with people who make you laugh,
- taking time for simple pleasures,
- sharing your life with a pet that loves you,
- keeping your work and living environment free of clutter,
- having work that is meaningful and connected to your vision for your life,
- maintaining a financial reserve.

In the strategies section, you will have an opportunity to take a look at your own list of energy drains, and identify ways in which you can replenish your energy. As you begin getting rid of things that drain your energy and building energy boosters into your life, you will be amazed at how energized you will feel and how well you will be able to focus on doing the things that support your priorities.

MANAGING YOUR TIME

A life skill that people often tell me they need to work on is time management. They frequently say:

"I just don't have enough time to get everything done."

"I just can't get caught up."

"The harder I work, the more behind I get."

111

In reality, the problem doesn't usually lie with how much time a person has or doesn't have. We all have exactly the same amount of time. What is important is the way we *use* our time.

Do you spend your time on what matters most to you? Or are you spending your time reacting to the demands around you? How often do you answer the phone when you are in the middle of an important project? How often do you agree to join another committee when you already have too little time to spend with your family?

Time management is not about doing more in less time; it's about doing what matters most in the time that you have. Time management is about living your life in alignment with your priorities and goals. It's about figuring out what you want to create in your life, and then allocating your time to create it!

> *"Time management is not about doing more in less time; it's about doing what matters most in the time that you have!"*

Let me take a moment to tell you about one thing that definitely does not work well for me—trying to do more in less time (multi-tasking). My daughter, Kim, and I have a running joke about which of us is multi-tasking the most while we are talking on the phone. For example, I may be looking over my E-mail on the computer, talking on the phone, and trying to respond non-verbally to a question my husband has just asked. The result is that I don't really pay very close attention to the E-mail I have received, the person I am talking to on the phone is feeling short-changed because my full attention isn't with him or her, and my husband is frustrated because he can't interpret my weird gesturing!

The essence of time management is best described in the following three caveats:

1. Identify your priorities.
2. Focus your time and energy on those priorities.
3. Delegate or eliminate responsibilities that are not in alignment with your priorities. This includes just saying "no."

There is a wonderful story about a man who, at age 55, made a discovery that changed his life. He realized that an average life span was approximately 75 years. After some calculations, he determined that he had approximately 1,000 Saturdays left. He went to the store, bought 1000 marbles and placed them in a jar. Each Saturday he removed a marble and threw it away. As the number of marbles left became fewer and fewer, he found that life seemed more precious. His priorities became very clear, and soon he was spending more time with those he loved. This story impressed me so strongly that I decided to do the same thing, using toothpicks instead of marbles. (They took up less space.) Removing one toothpick each Saturday keeps me very aware that our time is indeed limited, and that each day is a gift to be used wisely.

We know two things for sure about time:
- We won't have enough time for everything.
- We can make sure there is enough time for the important things.

In the strategies section, we will discuss specific techniques for identifying your priorities, mastering the power of focus, delegating certain responsibilities, and making sure that there is enough time for the important things.

MAINTAINING A SENSE OF HUMOR

Abraham Lincoln once said, "With the fearful strain that is on me night and day, if I did not laugh, I should die." Perhaps he had an inkling of what researchers know to be true today: A sense of humor and the laughter that accompanies it has powerful healing power. Humor is only recently starting to receive credit for its important role in our mental and physical health, and in our ability to rise above adversity. The kind of humor that I am referring to is an attitude of merriment, the ability to see the comical in things. It involves others in the fun, is based on caring and empathy, brings people closer together, and invites them to laugh. I am *not* referring to ridicule that is based on contempt and insensitivity, which often destroys confidence as a result of put-downs and making others the butt of a joke. Laughter at the expense (embarrassment) of others can be incredibly devastating to the person being laughed at. When we look at things from a perspective that includes humor, we decrease our feelings of stress and shift our focus to the positive. Many of us take ourselves so seriously. I will admit I'm one of the worst! I used to tackle tasks as if my life depended on getting those tasks done and getting them done perfectly! I rarely took time to smell the roses or share laughter with a friend.

What finally changed the way I looked at things was learning the following research-based facts from the Harvard Institute of Mind/Body Medicine:

- People who use humor as a coping strategy actually suffer less fatigue, tension, anger, depression, and confusion in response to stress.
- The stress-buffering effect of humor has been shown to enhance immune function.
- Humor improves mental well-being and is the sign of a healthy mind.
- Humor helps reduce conflict.
- Humor enhances memory and learning.
- Humor can be used as a means to create the relaxation response.

Humor is an ideal coping skill that helps us deal with adversity. It helps us relieve tension and be flexible when we are trying to cope with stressful situations. Humor promotes resilience by encouraging a broad and more relaxed perspective on life. Have you ever noticed the great bond you feel when sharing laughter with someone else? One of the best things I have accomplished is learning to laugh at myself. Humor is such a great connector of people, especially when we are chuckling together at our own humanness.

The really good news is that since humor is a cognitive function, it is under our control. As with any of the Life Skills for Effectiveness, humor is a learned skill that can become a part of your coping repertoire through repeated use. Not a bad way to invest your time! In Chapter 9, you will be given some strategies for increasing your ability to see humor in life and tap into some of life's funnier moments. The humor section might become your favorite part of the book!

> *"Humor promotes resilience by encouraging a broad and more relaxed perspective on life."*

MANAGING YOUR FINANCES

Sound financial management is a critical skill for promoting a sense of control and creating the life you want. No matter how much money you want to make or how much you need to live, the following five fundamental financial principles will help you achieve financial success:

- Know how much money you need to do what you want to do and have what you want to have.
- Live within your means.
- Build a reserve.
- Protect your most important assets (family, health, home, etc.).
- Make spending decisions based on your values.

In chapter 9 we will share several strategies to help you live these principles in your own life. For now, we will just provide an overview of each one.

> *"Sound financial management is a critical skill for promoting a sense of control and creating the life you want."*

Figure out how much money you need to do what you want to do and have what you want to have. By doing this, you are better able to make choices consistent with your values and needs. In our consumer culture, we tend to believe that more is better, so we work extended hours, trying to make more. Instead, start by calculating how much is enough— for you! You may be astounded to see how little you need in order to do what you want and have what you want.

Live within your means. Spend less than you make. When you live within your means you buy what you can afford with your current standard of living. When you spend beyond your means, you pay a huge interest penalty for the purchases you make and the debt burden grows deeper and deeper.

Build a reserve. Save for a rainy day. When you build a financial reserve, you have a bucket of money to draw from when times are tough, when unexpected expenses pile up, or when you want to take some time off to pursue a dream or special project. Without a reserve, you will always be living paycheck to paycheck and your flexibility to make different choices will be limited.

Protect your most important assets. Buy health insurance for all members of your family, even if they are healthy. One serious accident can wipe out years of savings. Select a life insurance instrument to provide for your family. Have a will and guardians for your children. Even a simple health insurance policy, life insurance policy, and will can go a long way toward protecting what matters most to you.

Make spending decisions based on your values. Spend only on the things that add value and energy to your life. Take some time to figure out what that is and then allocate your spending accordingly. If you value adventure, then allocating money to an adventure trip each year is probably more important than buying a big fancy house in the suburbs. If you value family, then spend your money on quality leisure activities for the family instead of fancy clothes. The choices are endless but the money supply is limited. Choose wisely.

When you aren't in control of your finances, it is easy to feel helpless. One of the top priorities in my own life, and one of the things that make me feel most empowered, is the freedom that comes from having lived by these five principles.

I am a firm believer that asking for help is essential when honing your financial management skills. There are many ways to educate yourself about money. Books such as Suze Orman's *The 9 Steps to Financial Freedom* are available for those of us who learn best from reading. Tapes and CDs are usually available as well. A wealth of information can be found on a daily basis in the Wall Street Journal or on Web sites such as Quicken.com. Another resource which can be key to improving both your financial wisdom and financial health is a trusted financial advisor. Well-planned financial management is an essential life skill if one is to attain financial freedom, achieve success, and have the ability to create the life you want to live.

NETWORKING EFFECTIVELY

We can achieve many things in life, but few of them can be accomplished alone. People need people! The best way to build your business, achieve your personal and professional goals, and make the process more fun and rewarding is by networking with others.

I've heard networking described as a full contact sport. You have to get out there and meet people. There is an old adage that it is not what you know but whom you know that is important. This is especially true in networking. The benefits are numerous, including business referrals. Many of the world's most successful business people have built their businesses by referral. My own business, success coaching, is definitely an example of building a business by referral. In addition, networking has provided me with numerous other connections for almost anything I might need, personally or professionally.

One thing that attracts me most about organized networks such as Business Network International or eWomen Network is what is known as a "Giver's Gain" mentality. Successful networkers approach networking with an attitude of asking "What can I give to others," but invariably end up gaining as much or more than they give.

I have come to believe that the ability to develop a well-rounded, effective network is a life skill that can play a key role in whether you typically feel empowered or helpless. Ivan R. Misner, Ph.D., CEO and Founder of Business Network International (BNI), has identified the following as components of a well-rounded network:

- **Information Network:** People in this network can support you with various decisions in your life. They are your access to information.
- **Support Network:** These are the people who will help you achieve any goal. They give you emotional, spiritual, physical, or financial support.
- **Referral Network:** This is the most important network for business. Empowered, successful people do business by referral. Your referral network is where many of your business

contacts will come from. Business people who have this network component fully developed may get 90% or more of their business by referral.

Most of us are not born networkers. We develop these skills through education, training, practice, and an attitude of commitment. As with other valuable life skills, we are most likely to benefit from networking if we devote the necessary time and resources to the development of a powerful network. In a wonderful conversation with David Alexander, Executive Director of the Regional Business Network International located in Atlanta, I learned that focusing on deepening relationships with people is one of the things that makes networking effective, and that certain characteristics contribute to the ability to deepen relationships. In a recent survey, more than 2,000 people throughout the United States, United Kingdom, Canada, and Australia were asked to select top networking traits. From the results, the top ten traits of a Master Networker were ranked in order of perceived importance. The survey results as shown below were about the same in all four countries, which tells us that the principles of good networking transcend national and cultural boundaries:

1. Follows up on referrals: 83%
2. Positive attitude: 76%
3. Enthusiastic: 64%
4. Trustworthy: 63%
5. Good listener: 63%
6. Networks always: 57%
7. Thanks people: 56%
8. Enjoys helping: 50%
9. Sincere: 46%
10. Works network: 45%

Notice that all the traits are relationship-oriented. Successful people operate in a relationship-based manner. Although our society has become quite enamored with efficiency—partly as a result of technology—good networkers focus on effectiveness. When you ask yourself the question, "Do I want a more *efficient* relationship with my spouse or significant other, or do I want a more *effective*, deep, loving, and caring relationship?" the answer is easy. We want to have a more *effective* relationship. I want an *efficient* relationship with my computer!

Just as in our personal relationships, we also want to have effective relationships in our networks. If our network relationships are treated with efficiency, they will never deepen. When I asked David why it is so important to strive to deepen our relationships with others in our network, he responded with an analogy. He asked, "What can you do with 211-degree water? Maybe boil an egg or make tea. What can you do with 212-degree water? You can boil the water and make steam. With that, you can power a civilization. It is impressive what a difference one degree can make." David suggests that as we start developing our networks, we always ask ourselves, "What is the degree of my relationship with the people I know, and what can I do to deepen those relationships to bring them to the boiling point?"

Remember, networking is a skill that can be consciously developed. In Chapter 9, we will do exercises that will help you start to build your network and hone your networking skills. In addition, I would highly recommend affiliating with a powerful networking organization such as Business Network International, which offers training classes on how to network and how to do word-of-mouth marketing, or eWomen Network.

IN A NUTSHELL

1. As you strengthen and develop your life skills, you increase your ability to respond effectively to obstacles and keep persevering toward your goal.

2. A sense of control plays a key role in the ability to rise above adversity and persevere toward your goals.

3. Helpful life skills:

   - Eliciting the relaxation response on a regular basis
   - Reframing your perspective on challenging situations
   - Communicating effectively
   - Renewing your energy
   - Managing your time
   - Managing your finances
   - Networking effectively

4. The body's "fight-or-flight" response occurs automatically in stressful situations. Consciously eliciting the relaxation response reduces or reverses many of the negative effects of chronic stress.

5. Reframing your perspective on challenging situations can help promote a sense of control.

6. Your perception of a situation is the major cause of how you respond emotionally, behaviorally, and physiologically.

7. Even though you may not be able to change your situation, you can change your frame of reference about the situation.

8. Every day you have a choice about the frame of reference from which you will view various situations.

9. You can greatly increase your sense of personal control and effectiveness by examining the way you communicate.

10. If you don't take time to renew your energy, you will quickly burn out. It is essential to make time for energy renewal.

11. Time management is not about doing more in less time; it's about doing what matters most in the time you have.

12. Humor is an ideal coping skill that helps us deal well with adversity. It promotes resilience by encouraging a broader and more relaxed perspective on life.

13. Sound financial management is a critical skill for promoting a sense of control and having the ability to create the life you want.

14. The ability to develop a well-rounded, effective network is a life skill that can play a key role in whether you typically feel empowered or helpless.

● ●

Lifestyle of Self-Care 5

The Model for Success is not a quick-fix program. It is not about reading a book, learning a couple of neat techniques and then setting the book aside. It is about the way you think, the way you feel, and the way you act, day in and day out. An essential part of achieving and enjoying success is developing the habit of maintaining a lifestyle of self-care. Developing a habit means that you do something on a regular basis for so long that it becomes "hard-wired" as a standard operating procedure in your life.

As we move toward our success goals, we seem to get busier and busier. As they say, time is money and efficiency is the name of the game. We rush through our lives, trying to complete our "to-do" lists, while at the same time taking on more and more. It rarely occurs to us that taking care of ourselves is as much a part of achieving and maintaining success as the "beat the clock" game that we play on a daily basis.

To make matters worse, many of us have never learned how to take care of ourselves, even if we wanted do. Women, in particular, have often been raised with the belief that they should take care of others, but it isn't okay to take care of themselves. Fortunately, there are some wonderful self-help books that not only give us permission to take care of ourselves, but offer excellent strategies as well. One of my favorite books on the subject of self-care is *Take Time for Your Life* by Cheryl Richardson. Another is *Coming Up for Air* by Beth Sawi.

For our purposes, a Lifestyle of Self-Care means that, in addition to your medical care, you include on a regular basis self-care strategies such as planning time for rest and relaxation, eating the right foods, exercising regularly, developing a strong social support system, and being in touch with your own spirituality. Have you ever caught yourself saying, "I don't have time for things like exercising or planned relaxation. I have a business to run and a family to take care of!" Take a moment to consider this idea:

"It is in developing a lifestyle of self-care that we renew our minds and our bodies on a regular basis, strengthen our resilience, and enhance our personal and professional effectiveness."

You don't have time *not* to include self-care in your lifestyle. It is in developing a lifestyle of self-care that we renew our minds and our bodies on a regular basis, strengthen our resilience, and enhance our personal and professional effectiveness. It is essential to have the knowledge and the tools you need to develop and put into practice a lifestyle of self-care that will support not only your success, but your physiological, psychological, and spiritual well-being as well. This book will provide you with both.

THE MODEL FOR SUCCESS: A MIND/BODY/ SPIRIT MODEL

The Model for Success is based, in part, on a mind/ body/spirit model of health and well-being. The term mind/body/spirit is used to describe the many complicated interactions that take place among your thoughts, your body, your spirit, and the outside world. Like the mind/body/spirit model, the Model for Success takes the position that success, health, and a sense of well-being depend on a multitude of factors including genetics, your health habits and lifestyle, your emotional state, your social supports, and your spiritual well-being. You

> *"The Model for Success takes the position that success, health, and a sense of well-being depend on a multitude of factors."*

are likely to achieve benefits from positive changes that you make in any one of these areas, but the best results are usually achieved when you address all of them. The strategies that accompany the Model for Success include the skills and techniques necessary to manage the stress-related challenges you face and to increase your overall effectiveness. The Lifestyle of Self-Care component is also designed to enhance your ability to maintain that effectiveness day in and day out by maximizing health benefits through lifestyle choices.

134

Why Is Healthy Lifestyle Important?

The awareness that mind and body interact helps you understand the significance of healthy lifestyle choices. We have discussed adversity at length. Adversity is often synonymous with stress, especially in the way that it affects your body. In the Model for Success, *stress* is defined as "the perception of threat to one's physical or psychological well-being, and the perception of being unable to cope." A *stressor* is "the perceived event that produces the feelings of stress."

Another definition of a stressor is "anything that requires change or adaptation." Some examples of common stressors are:

- fear of inability to do a job well,
- fear of job loss,
- anxiety because alarm fails to go off and you are running late for work,
- breakup of a long-time relationship,
- concern because your teenager is out much later than usual,
- the diagnosis of a serious illness.

135

It would be interesting to keep track of the number of stressors we experience every day. Remember, it is not what happens to you that causes the stress. It is your *perception* of what happens. For example, it is not the fact that your alarm clock failed to go off that causes you to feel stressed. It is what you thought about that event. If you believe that because you got up late, you are probably going to be late for work—and if you believe that being late for work might result in losing your job—you are probably going to feel a great deal of stress! You know that your body responds to stress with biochemical changes that prepare you to deal with threats or danger. You also know that because of these biochemical changes, you might experience such symptoms as elevated blood pressure, increased heart rate, more rapid breathing, heightened tension, and increased metabolism.

Because of the many negative effects of chronic stress, one of the goals of this book is to give you the tools you need to take control of how you respond to stress or adversity. We have discussed the importance of choosing the mindset with which you approach your life. It is equally important to maintain a lifestyle of self-care to help reduce and/or reverse the negative effects of stress.

A lifestyle of self-care refers to things that people can do for their own health and well-being. While there are many things we can do by way of self-care, some of the most important are:

> *"A lifestyle of self-care refers to things that people can do for their own health and well-being."*

- practice relaxation on a regular basis,
- exercise regularly,
- maintain a healthy diet,
- develop social support, and
- connect with your spiritual nature.

Reversing the Stress Response Through Conscious Relaxation

Because of the harmful effects of chronic stress on your health and well-being as well as your ability to

be productive and effective, it is essential to find ways
to control and
neutralize these
effects. One of the
things you can do is
become aware of
the importance of
relaxing your mind
and your body, and
practicing the life

> *"One of the things you can
> do is become aware of the
> importance of relaxing your
> mind and your body, and
> practicing the life skill of
> eliciting the relaxation
> response on a regular basis."*

skill of eliciting the relaxation response on a regular
basis. Most stress-hardy people try to relax for at least
15 minutes a day. Remember, the relaxation response
is your body's built-in mechanism for reversing the
physiological effects of the stress response.

In addition to consciously eliciting the relaxation
response, you can give yourself a wonderful gift by
learning to live in a more relaxed way. In our work-
centered culture, many of us believe that "our life is
our work," only to wake up one day wishing that we
had spent more time with those we love (including
our four-legged companions). I had a big dose of

that "wake up" experience when I was pushing myself to complete this book on the schedule I had created in my mind. I found myself retreating to my home office more and more in order to get one more paragraph, one more page, one more chapter written. Before I knew it, my wonderful months at our Florida home were over, and I hadn't even taken time out to play. I had severely short-changed my time with my husband, my family, my friends, and my dog. The only good news was that I had learned a valuable lesson, best expressed in this quote by Corita Kent:

"Life is a succession of moments. To live each one is to succeed."

I was approaching life as if success equaled the completion of a book—period! But at the end of four months, it had become very clear to me that in my life, success isn't achieved by writing a book. I will achieve success to the extent that I live fully and with enjoyment each and every moment. This doesn't mean that I don't enjoy working. I do—very much! But I enjoy it more, and am more productive, when I work, play, take time for self-care, and enjoy the simple pleasures that life has to offer. A lifestyle of self-care means that you give yourself the gift of self-care, including relaxation, on a regular basis.

Regular Exercise

> *"Exercise is an excellent means of gaining some control over the negative effects of adversity and chronic stress."*

You may find that just reading the word "exercise" makes you shudder. The fact is, however, that lack of physical movement and lack of fresh air cause exhaustion and are major contributors to stress. Exercise is an excellent means of gaining some control over the negative effects of adversity and chronic stress. People who are resilient and have developed a stress-hardy personality tend to exercise on a regular basis. Studies have shown that exercise will decrease anxiety and tension, and that it is an excellent means of reducing the effects of stress. When your body is in a "fight-or-flight" state of arousal, exercise provides a natural outlet and allows the body to return to its normal equilibrium by releasing natural chemicals that build up during stress. Appropriate exercise has been found to:

- minimize the risk of heart attacks,
- increase good (HDL) cholesterol,
- promote weight control,
- temper back pain, and
- increase longevity.

Exercise is good for your self-esteem, too. I take my dog for long walks every morning, even when I'm tempted to roll over and sleep in. Just by getting out and exercising, I notice that my mood brightens, I feel a sense of pride in myself, I am able to keep a handle on my weight, and—the best part—I get a lot of grateful doggie kisses.

If you are thinking that exercising sounds like a good idea, there are certain questions that need to be answered:
- What kind of exercise?
- How much?
- For what purpose?

141

If maximum well-being is your goal, exercise that enhances your cardiovascular endurance is the best choice. Aerobic exercise such as running, walking, bicycling, or swimming, will help you achieve cardiovascular benefits that decrease your risk of heart disease (i.e. lowering cholesterol and high blood pressure, losing fat, and increasing circulation to your heart). The 1993 President's Council recommended dynamic movement, twenty minutes at a time or longer, at an intensity of 60% of your maximal heart rate or greater, on a regular basis— at least three times a week.

Research has shown that rather than pushing yourself too hard, you can benefit significantly from such activities as a brisk walk, a swim, a favorite sport, dancing, or raking leaves. When you exercise at a range of 50 to 60 percent of the heart's maximum capacity, you can achieve cardiovascular benefits and reduce symptoms of stress. You can accomplish this through normal and enjoyable activities that are aerobic, but not necessarily very demanding on discipline.

An accepted definition of maximal exercise capacity is "the most exercise you can do before fatigue makes you stop." The heart rate you obtain with maximal exercise is your maximal heart rate. Your goal, however, is not to try to obtain maximal capacity, but to select a target heart rate that will provide the benefits you desire. Your target heart rate will be based on your maximal heart rate.

In the strategies section of this book, you will learn to calculate your maximal heart rate and be provided with ideas for starting your exercise program.

Maintain A Healthy Diet

> *"Success, health, and well-being are the results of both physical and mental factors, including a healthy diet."*

Success, health, and well-being are the results of both physical and mental factors, including finding a healthy balance of essential nutrients and caloric intake. Good eating habits contribute to a healthy body, and can help prevent or control high blood pressure, heart disease, indigestion, constipation, hypoglycemia, diabetes, and obesity. Healthy eating has also been found to reduce irritability, headaches, and fatigue.

Americans, as well as people of other cultures, often eat to celebrate holidays and other special events, including passages of life. Meals provide an opportunity to relax and socialize and can often help to reduce stress. Unfortunately, we often fail to choose food that is nutritionally sound.

Moderation is the building block of sound nutrition and a stress-free diet. Americans tend to eat too much red meat, poultry with the skin, regular cheese, ice cream, and other whole milk dairy products, and fried food. As a result, we often fail to choose enough fruits, vegetables, legumes (beans, lentils, and peas) and whole grain products. The USDA food guide pyramid provides a good guide to a healthy diet.

The good news is that you are in charge of your eating habits. In the strategies section, you will find guidelines for creating and maintaining a healthy diet. *Bon appétit!*

Social Support: Isolation vs. Connectedness

Have you ever noticed how much better you feel when you can talk about a troublesome situation with a friend? Stress studies have repeatedly shown that the greatest buffer against stress is social support. Researchers sometimes define social support as the degree to which our social needs are met through our interaction with other people. This includes feeling like you can count on others for help and having others who will truly listen to you (and you, in turn, listen to them.) When you have social support you feel cared about, valued, and have a sense of belonging. You have access to advice and guidance, and sometimes even physical or material assistance. In addition to these benefits, there are also health benefits. When people have a healthy social support network, they typically feel a sense of well-being and a greater sense of control. Researchers believe that the sense of well-being and control that accompanies healthy social ties acts as a buffer against stress by

> *"When people have a healthy social support network, they typically feel a sense of well-being and a greater sense of control."*

protecting people from the diseases that stress often causes. Just as feeling isolated has been shown to be detrimental to health, a feeling of connectedness has been shown in repeated studies to be healing. In short, isolation has been found to suppress the immune system, while connectedness has been found to enhance the immune system.

The comfort of another human being may be one of nature's most powerful antidotes to stress. Dr. James Lynch, a well-known researcher in the field of social support, sums up his results as follows: "The mandate to "love your neighbor as you love yourself" is not just a moral mandate. It is a physiological mandate. Caring is biological. One thing you get from caring for others is that you're not lonely; and the more connected you are to life, the healthier you are."

My favorite research study that illustrates the connection among social support, health, well-being, and a sense of control over one's life is a study that was conducted in a close-knit Italian-American community in Roseto, Pennsylvania. Researchers were interested in how lifestyle affected health and longevity, particularly as related to heart disease. The men who lived in Roseto had only one-sixth as many incidences of heart disease and deaths from heart disease as random population groups in the United States. The incidence among women was even less. When examining the lifestyles of the Roseto residents, researchers expected to find that they ate primarily health foods (bean sprouts), that they didn't smoke, and that they exercised rigorously. What a surprise they had when they found, instead, that most of those who lived in Roseto tended to be carnivorous, cigarette-smoking people with sedentary life styles. They had at least an average incidence of the risk factors such as cigarette smoking, obesity, high blood pressure, and stress. The researchers concluded that the major protective factor—the thing that was different among Roseto residents—was that in the community of Roseto, a prime value was relationship with others. People tended not to take on extra jobs or move away from Roseto to seek better employment. When interviewed, residents would say things like, "I want to spend time with my family and friends. We want to be involved in each other's lives." The social structure of Roseto reflected old-world values of cohesiveness and unconditional support within the community. Sadly, as researchers continued to monitor the residents of Roseto, they found that as the younger generation grew up and began severing ties with the old-world traditions, the health of Roseto residents began to decline.

It is alarming to note that national statistics in many ways reflects those of Roseto. In a lecture by Dr. Joan Borysenko, it was noted that in 1945, 85% of United States residents lived in extended families. By 1993, only 3% of the population lived in an extended family. People were moving to where the jobs were. People today are more likely to live alone, less likely to be married, and less likely to belong to a social organization. Unfortunately, we are paying for our increasing isolation with our health, as shown in statistics on heart attacks, high blood pressure, ulcers, death rates, and others. It appears that one of the main reasons social support contributes so significantly to good health is that it improves the immune system, even during times of great stress. It also appears that a strong social support system leads to a greater sense of control over our lives. From the research, we know that a sense of control also increases our resilience and our effectiveness. Perhaps it is time for all of us to recognize the importance of social support in our own lives, and begin finding ways to strengthen our own social support networks.

SPIRITUALITY

Spirituality can be defined as a sense of connection to our own true nature, to other people, and to a power greater than ourselves. It is your sense of connection and your commitment to your values that give you a sense of meaning and purpose. Perhaps this is what researcher Suzanne Oullette refers to when she speaks of commitment as one of the characteristics of stress-hardy people. When you live your life and choose your words and actions based on your commitment to your value system, you feel renewed, strengthened, and centered. The desire to serve others and a sense of personal mission in life are at the heart of spirituality.

> *"When you live your life and choose your words and actions based on your commitment to your value system, you feel renewed, strengthened, and centered."*

Spirituality means different things to different people. Some think of spirituality as a state of well-being which encompasses more than just the absence of disease. Others think of spirituality as being at peace with self and environment. Still others think of spirituality as giving of self for a purpose or value, having a sense of mission, finding meaning and wisdom in here-and-now difficulties, enjoying the process of growth, and having a vision of one's potential. Your spiritual nature is never about judging or putting others down, as we sometimes tend to do in the name of religion or spirituality. Judging alienates us from others rather than promoting a sense of connection. Instead of promoting hope, it promotes discouragement. In short, your spiritual nature is the essence of loving- kindness.

Getting in touch with your spiritual nature means knowing and honoring what gives your life meaning and purpose. You may center on family relationships, or humanitarian efforts, or simply taking care of a plant. Whatever you choose, it can serve as a powerful motivator toward personal accomplishment.

> *"Getting in touch with your spiritual nature means knowing and honoring what gives your life meaning and purpose."*

Without a sense of meaning and purpose, the will to live is often lost. That is why developing a vision for your life and taking time to be clear about your personal mission in life is so important. Connecting with your spirituality means reaching deep within yourself to understand the core of who you are. You get in touch with what gives your life meaning and purpose, and recommit to it frequently.

The message on Peter Russell's answering machine—"Who are you and what do you want" — reminds each of us to ask ourselves, "Who am I and what do I want?" When you ask yourself those two simple questions on a regular basis, you connect with your spiritual nature, with what is deeply important to you, and with what gives your life meaning and purpose. People who have made that connection to their spiritual nature—who have that sense of meaning and purpose—are better able to weather crises and adversity. They see life differently and they live life differently. They have the sense of purpose and the broad perspective that allows them to stop focusing on themselves, and start focusing on others. They are not defeated by crisis. In seeing the big picture, they realize that an adverse event in their lives is not necessarily a catastrophe, but rather, a challenge that can be used for personal growth. Last, but not least, one of the remarkable benefits of being closely connected to your spiritual nature is that it is a great source of energy. Try charging up your life by "plugging in" to your spiritual nature.

When you live a lifestyle of self-care you empower yourself. Instead of allowing yourself to be

> *"Being closely connected to your spiritual nature is a great source of energy."*

victimized by the "rat race" that so many of us get caught up in, you RISE ABOVE IT. You are pro-active, and you take control of your life by living from a core value of mental, physical, and spiritual well-being.

IN A NUTSHELL

1. A Lifestyle of Self-Care means that, in addition to your medical care, you include on a regular basis self-care strategies such as:
   - ✓ planning time for rest and relaxation,
   - ✓ eating the right foods,
   - ✓ exercising regularly,
   - ✓ developing a strong social support system, and
   - ✓ being in touch with your own spirituality.

153

2. It is in developing a lifestyle of self-care that we renew our minds and our bodies on a regular basis, strengthen our resilience, and enhance our personal and professional effectiveness.

3. The Model for Success takes the position that success, health, and a sense of well-being depend on a multitude of factors including genetics, your health habits and lifestyle, your emotional state, your social supports, and your spiritual well-being.

4. The awareness that mind and body interact helps you understand the significance of healthy lifestyle choices.

5. In the Model for Success, stress is defined as "the perception of threat to one's physical or psychological well-being, and the perception of being unable to cope." A stressor is defined as "the perceived event that produces the feelings of stress."

6. Because of the many negative effects of chronic stress, it is important to acquire the tools and strategies you need to take control of how you respond to stress and adversity.

7. A Lifestyle of Self-Care refers to things that people can do for their own health and well-being.

8. A Lifestyle of Self-Care means that you give yourself the gift of self-care on a regular basis.

9. One of the things you can do is become aware of the importance of relaxing your mind and your body, and implement this life skill on a regular basis.

10. The relaxation response is your body's built-in mechanism for reversing the physiological effects of the stress response.

11. Exercise is an excellent means of gaining some control over the negative effects of adversity and chronic stress.

12. If maximum well-being is your goal, exercise that enhances your cardiovascular endurance is an excellent choice.

13. Success, health, and well-being are the results of both physical and mental factors.

14. Social support is often defined by researchers as the degree to which our social needs are met through our interaction with other people.

15. When you have social support, you feel cared about, valued, and have a sense of belonging.

16. When people have a healthy social support network, they typically feel a sense of well-being and a greater sense of control.

17. Strong social support increases not only a sense of control, but our resilience and effectiveness as well.

18. Just as feeling isolated has been shown to be detrimental to health, a feeling of connectedness has been shown to be healing.

19. People today are more likely to live alone, less likely to be married, and less likely to belong to a social organization. Unfortunately, we are paying for our increasing isolation with our health.

20. Spirituality can be defined as a sense of connection to our own true nature, to other people, and to a power greater than ourselves.

21. When you live your life and choose your words and actions based on your commitment to your value

system, you feel renewed, strengthened, and centered.

22. Getting in touch with your spiritual nature means knowing and honoring what gives your life meaning and purpose.

23. Being closely connected to your spiritual nature is a great source of energy.

• •

Conscious Endeavor 6

There is a wonderful quote by Henry David Thoreau that says:

"I know of no more encouraging fact than the unquestionable ability of man to elevate his life by conscious endeavor."

You may be wondering, "What in the world is conscious endeavor?" I think of conscious endeavor as living your life with great awareness, consciously making choices about what you value in life, and the goals you will strive for, and accepting responsibility for how you will respond when adversity comes your way. We elevate our lives to a higher plane when we take responsibility for our own success and happiness. It is so easy to go through life making mechanical responses to situations.We simply *react* based on old habits, old beliefs, destructive and/or limiting self-talk, and old ways of doing things that may no longer be serving us well. We don't consciously think about our responses— we just react. It is a much greater challenge to make a commitment to elevate your life with conscious endeavor—to be *proactive* by consciously giving thought to how we wish to respond to the people and events in our lives.

Going through life is something like creating a recipe for a cake. In both cases, you can create something very ordinary—very unremarkable—or you can design something truly magnificent. In both cases, you also have the opportunity to consciously take responsibility for the quality of the product (your cake or your life), by wisely choosing the ingredients you want to include and those you want to exclude.

The key words are *consciously* and *responsibility.* You consciously take responsibility when you know and accept that you are the one who will pro-actively determine the quality of your life. You do this, in part, by consciously choosing your responses to people and situations in your life. You don't have to respond to life based on old habits. You can take the responsibility to make conscious choices in life, knowing the alternatives available to you.

> *"You consciously take responsibility when you know and accept that you determine the quality of your life, and consciously choose your response to people and situations."*

Just as you might consciously choose to add or eliminate ingredients from an old family recipe, you may also consciously take responsibility for adding or excluding life ingredients that depart from your usual way of doing things. For example, some people deal with problems by ignoring them. Others deal with them by blaming others. You may realize that both ignoring and blame are ingredients that don't serve you well, so you take the responsibility to consciously exclude ignoring and blame from your life recipe. On the other hand, some people seem to model compassion for others, realizing that hateful actions are often just a mask for emotional pain. You can make the choice to include compassion as an ingredient in your recipe for life. These are both examples of living with conscious endeavor.

Living your life with conscious endeavor is perhaps the most significant strategy for strengthening your ability to overcome adversity and achieving success. When we live with conscious endeavor, we recognize that everything is a choice, and we consciously make the choices that will elevate our lives and help us rise above the challenges that come our way.

Exercise #1

Think of an adverse or challenging situation that has occurred in your life in the last month or two. Write it down.

_____

_____

Using the scale below, circle the number that best describes your response to that situation. Was your response reactive and possibly destructive, or proactive and constructive?

Reactive/Unconscious   **Proactive/Conscious Choice**

1   2   3   4   5   6   7   8   9   10

Did you consciously choose your response?

Yes_____ No_____

If you reacted rather than consciously choosing your response, a good start toward living with conscious endeavor is to develop the habit of quickly identifying stressful, potentially aversive situations, and becoming aware of how you typically respond. As you think about your usual responses, ask yourself whether your responses are more toward the reactive end of the scale, offering blame or withdrawing, or are you already taking responsibility for consciously choosing your responses, searching for win-win solutions or examining what you can productively do?

Write down how you typically respond:

_____

_____

Exercise #2:

This next exercise is designed to increase your awareness of situations that have the potential to trigger a reactive response. When you become aware, you have the opportunity to take responsibility and choose a more constructive response. This week, start identifying situations that "push your hot button" or trigger a stress response. As stressful or challenging situations occur, write down a brief description of the situation. Don't rate your response yet or identify a proactive response you could choose. We will do that later.

<u>**Your Response**</u>

<u>Situation:</u>   **<u>Reactive</u>   <u>Proactive</u>**

_____ 1 2 3 4 5 6 7 8 9 10

A proactive response I could choose: _____

_____

<u>Situation:</u>   **<u>Your Response</u>**

_____ 1 2 3 4 5 6 7 8 9 10

A proactive response I could choose:

_____

Situation: **Your Response**

_____   **1 2 3 4 5 6 7 8 9 10**

A proactive response I could choose:

_____

Now think about how you dealt with the situation. Did you react to the trigger or did you catch yourself and make a conscious choice about how you responded? In the column next to the situation, rate your response by circling the number that best represents where your response fell on the continuum (reactive vs. proactive.) Now write down a more proactive response you could choose.

Selecting a more proactive response is a matter of being aware that we have choice, identifying our pattern, and then creatively coming up with alternative responses that work for us.

The ability to consciously think about how one is going to respond, weigh alternatives, and choose the most effective response is a unique characteristic of humans. Sometimes we use this ability to give thought to our responses, and sometimes we simply react. When we are responding or reacting to events in our lives without thinking about our responses, the process looks like this:

S ➡ R

There is no thought, no weighing of alternatives, no conscious choice based on which of the responses available to us would be most effective.

However, when we use our ability to weigh the situation and choose what we believe to be the most effective response, the process looks like this:

S ➡ Thought ➡ R

Stimulus **Conscious Choice** **Response**
of Response

Because so many of our responses or reactions were learned in childhood, it is easy to fall back on habitual ways of doing things. In my family, when I did something that upset my mother, she would walk off in a huff, hoping that by punishing me in this way, I would come around to her way of thinking. Unfortunately, I discovered that I was reacting in this same way when my children did something that I didn't like. Like my mother, I walked off in a huff, hoping for an apology and/or change in behavior from my children. To my knowledge, walking off in a huff wasn't an effective response by my mother when I was a child, nor was it effective with my children. It was simply a conditioned response that I learned early in childhood. Conflict was the stimulus, walking off in a huff was the conditioned response. I had never stopped to consider that I could choose a more effective response. Fortunately, what I finally learned was that it is far more productive to stick around and try to work things out rather than to walk away from my problems. That response is now my choice!

We have many other choices to make in our lives in addition to responses to people and events. In the past, choices about where we would live, what career we would pursue, and what religion we would practice were often made for us by family tradition and local customs. However, in his excellent book, *The Art of Living Consciously,* Nathaniel Branden points out that in today's world we are obligated to make more and more conscious choices for ourselves, including the values by which we live, the goals we pursue, and what we define as success. Regardless of whether success means achieving material wealth, emotional fulfillment, or spiritual enhancement, the formula for success is the same— continuous learning and making conscious choices throughout our life.

For many of us, the events of September 11, 2001 greatly increased the importance of living with conscious endeavor. We suddenly found ourselves looking critically at and challenging old beliefs that have shaped our choices and our actions for years. Living with conscious endeavor requires, as a beginning, a willingness to

"Living with conscious endeavor requires a willingness to accept that old ways may no longer be serving us well."

accept the fact that our old ways of doing things and some of our old beliefs may no longer be serving us well. We may wish to begin consciously reprioritizing and making conscious choices about our careers and our personal lives. Or we may be reminded to reinvest in relationships by deepening our commitment to those we

> *"In essence, it is all about awareness and choices."*

care about. We may consciously choose to recommit to our vision for our lives and to the success of a career we love. In essence, it is all about awareness and choices.

Every day each of us has a new opportunity to understand what it means to take responsibility for the quality of our lives. The awareness of our ability to make conscious choices when faced with difficult situations allows us to make choices that are consistent with our values and goals, and to re-focus our energy and effort on what matters most.

In Chapter 8 you will learn to consciously develop a mindset of hardiness, a mindset that helps you bounce back from stress and adversity. You will also learn to identify and reframe self-talk that is negative, limiting, and self-destructive. The purpose of this chapter is simply to increase your *awareness* of the unique human capacity to recognize quickly when a situation triggers a reactive response from you, and to enhance your ability to weigh alternatives and make conscious *choices* about how you will respond.

"That's Just The Way I Am!"

When I am talking with clients, they sometimes say things like, "My family members have always been hot-tempered. That's just the way we are," or "I get angry at the drop of a hat. That's just the way I am!" These clients don't realize that they have control over their emotions and their responses. In fact, they sometimes even reject the idea that they might be able to change by taking responsibility for their attitudes, emotions, and responses. Openness to changing your perspective and a willingness to hold yourself accountable for making needed changes are essential for living with conscious endeavor, for improving your resilience (hardiness), and for moving you toward successful achievement of your goals and dreams.

The following two exercises work well for increasing your awareness and strengthening your ability to choose effective responses when faced with challenges and roadblocks.

Exercise #3:

Take time to have a little talk with yourself. Ask yourself these questions:

1. What old, destructive beliefs, attitudes, self-talk, or behaviors are getting in the way of my making constructive pro-active responses?
   Example: If I don't know the answer, people will think I am stupid.

2. What is the benefit to me of changing my responses?
   Examples: I don't have to always know the answer. Reduced stress. Fewer arguments.

3. What am I willing to do to change my attitudes, self-talk, or behaviors that aren't serving me well?

Exercise #4

Identify a challenging situation that you are facing right now.

_____

Now ask yourself these questions:

1. What am I trying to accomplish? What do I want the outcome of this situation to be?

_____

_____

_____

2. How are my reactive responses coloring my view of the alternatives or options I see?

_____

_____

_____

3. What other options or alternatives could I take?

_____

_____

_____

4. Now list the pro's and con's of each option.

OPTIONS	PRO'S	CON'S
A. _____	_____	_____
B. _____	_____	_____
C. _____	_____	_____
D. _____	_____	_____

5. Finally, ask yourself: Which of these options would maximize the likelihood of achieving an outcome I want? Which responses will improve the quality of my life?

_____

_____

Strengthen Your Response-Ability

You commit to conscious endeavor when you commit to strengthening your response-ability. Choose your responses wisely. Use the ideas and exercises in this book to help you recognize when you may not be responding very

> *"You commit to conscious endeavor when you commit to strengthening your response-ability."*

effectively to people and situations in your life, and begin developing strategies to choose responses that would be more constructive and more effective in achieving your dreams and goals.

● ●

Vision Strategy 7

CREATE A CLEAR VISION FOR YOUR LIFE

Having a clear vision for your life is critical to the ability to consistently overcome adversity and achieve success in your life. Why?

- Your vision keeps before you your mental picture of the life you want.
- Your vision gives you hope.
- Your vision motivates you when the going gets tough.

> *"Having a clear vision for your life is critical to your ability to consistently overcome adversity and achieve success."*

In his book, *The 7 Habits of Highly Effective People*, Stephen Covey teaches us to "Begin with the end in mind." That is what having a vision is all about. Your vision provides the roadmap for your choices and your actions. You start creating your vision when you begin

179

to clarify who you want to be in this world, and what you want your life to represent to others. The following is a condensed version of one of my favorite Covey exercises for starting to think about your vision for your life. I call it "The Funeral Exercise." I have found this exercise to be very effective for clarifying what I valued in life and what I wanted my life to stand for, personally and professionally.

> Imagine that you are going to the funeral of someone you cared about very deeply. As you arrive, friends and family are sharing the sorrow of losing—but the joy of having known—this person. You suddenly realize that you are attending your own funeral at the end of a long life. People have gathered to honor you and share their love for you and appreciation for your life.

> There are to be four speakers at the funeral. The first is someone from your family, immediate or extended. The second speaker is someone who can share what it is like to have known you as a friend. The third speaker is from your work and the fourth is from your church or a community organization to which

you have devoted time. What would you like for each of these people to say about you? What was it like to be your family member, or your friend, or your work associate? What would they say characterized you? What achievements would they remember? What difference would they say you have made in their lives?

As you answer these questions, you will actually be creating your vision for yourself as a person, a family member, a friend, a work associate, and a community member. You will, in fact, be beginning with the end in mind.

Exercise #1:

Write down what you would want each of these people to be able to say when describing you:

Family Members:

_____

_____

Friends:

_____

_____

Work Associates:

_____

_____

Community Members:

_____

_____

When you have a clear and compelling vision, it has tremendous power to motivate you and keep you focused, day in and day out. When you ask yourself the right questions, you become clearer about your vision and what you want your life to look like.

Exercise #2:

Ask yourself these questions and jot down your answers:

1. What do I want my life to be all about?

_____

2. To what am I committed?

_____

3. What are my values?

_____

4. Does my vision reflect my values?

_____

182

Exercise #3:

Allow yourself to relax and dream for a moment of how life could be for you. Allow yourself to consider the possibilities. Think about the following questions and then journal below detailing your dreams. Remove the Critic from your head and allow yourself to dream freely.

Questions:

a. Where do you want to live? What kind of home do you want? Who do you want to live with?

b. What work do you want to do each day? With whom do you want to work? How many hours do you want to work?

c. How much money do you want to make? What do you want to have? What do you want to accomplish in your life?

d. Who do you want to spend time with? What do you want to do in your free time?

Journal Critic-free:

_____

_____

_____

Life Areas

When thinking about our vision for our lives and what is important, meaningful, and valuable to us, we sometimes overlook big areas of our lives in which we need to make changes. Our lives are made up of many facets including career, relationships, emotional and physical health, spiritual well-being, community contributions, and fun and adventure.

The first step toward making change in your life is to identify clearly what you want each of these life areas to look like. As you begin shaping your vision for your life, use the format in Exercise #4 to help you look at the major aspects of your life. You will be able to see which areas you might be neglecting, and begin to recognize more clearly what is important to you.

Exercise #4:

Take a moment to clarify what success means to you in each of the following areas by asking yourself these questions about each area: What does success mean to me in this area? What changes do

I need to make in this area of my life? What results am I hoping to achieve by making changes? What will I be like when I make the changes I want to make? What will my life be like? Write down your answers.

Career:
I will know I am successful when:

_____

_____

The changes I need to make in this area are:

_____

_____

The results I hope to achieve by making these changes are:

_____

_____

What will I be like when I make these changes?

_____

_____

What will my life be like when I make these changes?

_____

_____

185

Relationships:

I will know I am successful when:

_____

_____

The changes I need to make in this area are:

_____

_____

The results I hope to achieve by making these changes are:

_____

_____

What will I be like when I make these changes?

_____

_____

What will my life be like when I make these changes?

_____

_____

Emotional and Physical Health:

I will know I am successful when:

_____

_____

The changes I need to make in this area are:

_____

_____

The results I hope to achieve by making these changes are:

_____

_____

What will I be like when I make these changes?

_____

_____

What will my life be like when I make these changes?

_____

_____

<u>Spiritual Well-being:</u>

I will know I am successful when:

_____

_____

The changes I need to make in this area are:

_____

_____

The results I hope to achieve by making these changes are:

_____

_____

What will I be like when I make these changes?

_____

_____

What will my life be like when I make these changes?

_____

_____

Community Contribution:

I will know I am successful when:

_____

_____

The changes I need to make in this area are:

_____

_____

The results I hope to achieve by making these changes are:

_____

_____

What will I be like when I make these changes?

_____

_____

What will my life be like when I make these changes?

_____

_____

Fun and Adventure:

I will know I am successful when:

_____

_____

The changes I need to make in this area are:

_____

_____

The results I hope to achieve by making these changes are:

_____

_____

What will I be like when I make these changes?

_____

_____

What will my life be like when I make these changes?

_____

_____

Vision Provides Meaning and Purpose

Feeling committed to a vision for the future provides a sense of meaning and purpose in our lives. As we have seen, the life of Dr. Victor Frankl provides a powerful example of the importance of having a vision, of having a sense of meaning and purpose. Dr. Frankl, tortured in the Nazi prison camps, never knew from one day to the next whether he would be one of those who would be sent to the gas ovens. As he endured the horrors of his circumstances, he realized that he had the freedom—perhaps man's greatest freedom—to decide how his experience was going to affect him. He had the power to choose how he would respond to his circumstances. How he ultimately did respond was inspired by his *vision* for his life. Dr. Frankl pictured himself in a classroom, lecturing to students about the lessons he had learned in the prison. His clear vision for his future after he was released from the death camp provided the passion that motivated him and gave him hope.

As he helped people find meaning and purpose in their lives, he became the source of great inspiration for many others in the prison camp.

A sense of meaning and purpose, and a clear vision of life as you want it to be, serve not only as powerful motivators, but also as a compass, providing a sense of direction in your life. As you begin to tie your vision—and ultimately your goals—to the things you value deeply in life, you will be more passionate about what you are trying to achieve. When you are passionate about what you are trying to achieve, you will be more motivated, more empowered to persevere, and more likely to make your vision a reality.

Core Values

Your vision for yourself includes honoring what are known as core values. Your core values are at the heart of who you are. They define your essence, those characteristics and values that lie deep within your heart and form the center of your life. The following list represents a variety of core values. Take a moment to look at this list and circle your core values.

What do you want to live, teach, or represent in this world? What do you feel passionate about? Feel free to list other core values that fit for you.

Integrity	Spirituality	Sense of accomplishment	
Health	Tenderness	Communications	Joy
Triumph	Kindness	Awareness	Character
Education	Consciousness	Connectedness	Discovery
Elegance	Fairness	Empathy	Peace
Freedom	Magnificence	Supportiveness	Forgiveness
Excellence	Humor	Responsiveness	Work
Making a difference		Challenge	Other _____

Exercise #5:

Write down the three values that most matter to you:

_____

_____

_____

Be sure these values are reflected in your vision for your life.

Use Your Resources

As you think about what is important to you, you may want to include others in this process. Talk to some of your best friends about what's important to them. Talk to your co-workers. Talk to children. Call your parents or grandparents and ask what has been important at various stages in their lives. Talk to devotees of different faiths. Talk to acquaintances in other professions. Put simply, talk to as many people as you can from as many walks of life as possible in order to broaden your scope about what is important to you. Understanding their perspective will help you expand and clarify your vision for yourself.

Exercise #6

Identify five people with whom you might want to talk about what is important to them in their lives. Make a note of when you will contact them.

Person I Wish to Contact   Contact Date

_____   _____

_____   _____

_____   _____

_____   _____

_____   _____

Exercise #7:

To close out the chapter on *Vision*, ask yourself: "What five things would I want to be sure to do if I knew I had only one more year to live?" List them below:

1. _____

2. _____

3. _____

4. _____

5. _____

Dare To Dream

People often place limitations on themselves when creating a vision for their lives. Stretch yourself. Dare to dream. Think big! And one final thing—this vision is just the beginning. Stick with it. Update it as your life evolves. Keep it in front of you. A clear vision provides hope. It creates a passion for living. It is the light on your path to success.

Create A Mindset of Hardiness

"It is difficult to overestimate the power of perceived control. Without it hope and action are crushed. With it, lives can be transformed and destinies fulfilled."
Paul Stoltz, Ph.D. in *The Adversity Quotient: Turning Obstacles Into Opportunities*

All of us have a mindset—a frame of reference from which we look at our lives. The question is, "Do we have a mindset that gives us the sense of control we need to rise above adversity and achieve success?" Some of us will be able to answer "yes" to that question. But many of us will realize that we need to make some changes in our current attitudes and beliefs in order to become more flexible and more resilient in difficult times.

Change is always a challenge and may feel somewhat uncomfortable. But if you are committed to making changes in your mindset that will strengthen your resilience, improve your coping abilities, and help you achieve success, it can be done.

Creating Your Mindset of Hardiness

The creation of a Mindset of Hardiness is a strong, proactive step you can take to ensure that you have the resilience to rise above stress and adversity. It is your mindset—your attitudes and beliefs—that determines whether you feel the perceived control that Paul Stoltz refers to in the quote above. As you will recall, we are defining stress as a *perception* of threat to our physical and psychological well-being, and the *perception* of being unable to cope. Perception is the key word. Fortunately, perception—how we view a situation and our ability to cope—can be changed. When we learn to alter our perceptions, we can change how we experience and respond to a stressful event. In other words, we can increase our perception of having some control over situations, and thereby become much more resilient.

Re-visiting the Basics

In Chapter 2, we looked at the continuum between helplessness and empowerment. A sense of empowerment is really having that sense of perceived control. It is your mindset that is going to determine where you fall on this continuum—whether you have a sense of perceived control or feel helpless.

EMPOWERMENT:
(Perceived control; my actions can affect the outcome.)

10

9

8

7

6

ADVERSITY

_____

5

4

3

2

1

HELPLESSNESS:
(Perceived lack of control; nothing I can do will affect the outcome of this situation).

The line in the continuum represents the occurrence of adversity. Our goal is to **RISE ABOVE IT** toward empowerment. Most of us don't usually feel totally helpless, which would place us at the bottom of the continuum. Nor do we often feel totally empowered and totally in control, which would rank us at level 10. We usually fall somewhere in between. Since we need that sense of empowerment—that feeling of being in control of challenging situations—our goal is to develop a mindset that will enable us to function near the top of the Empowerment Continuum most of the time.

Think about every person you have ever observed as they took on overwhelming, "against the odds" challenges. Consider the outstanding people who have changed the world, or those who have overcome life-threatening illnesses. Without exception, these people felt empowered. They started with a belief that their actions would make a difference—a perception of control. The more each of us moves toward empowerment, the more hopeful, resilient, motivated, and successful we become.

A SENSE OF CONTROL

A sense of control and empowerment begins with the belief that something can be done to improve the outcome of a difficult situation. When you have that perception, you will feel hopeful and are likely to take action, to persevere despite

> *"A sense of control and empowerment begins with the belief that something can be done to improve the outcome of a difficult situation."*

the adversity. When you take action, you are more likely to experience some degree of success that will motivate you to take more action.

Here's an example: Recently I lost a folder containing the outline for a major presentation that I was to make within a couple of weeks. Also in the folder was an audio-tape that I had made while brainstorming ideas for the presentation with my partner, Abby. My first reaction was to panic. My self-talk was, "How could I be so stupid? I'll never get this presentation reconstructed in time. I'll never be able to do the presentation." But almost before the negative self-talk had time to kick in, I switched gears and started taking control of the situation. I arranged with Abby to tape another session in which we would reconstruct the presentation. Then I would block out extra time to rework the presentation. While this situation wasn't the major adversity we sometimes encounter, it was terribly upsetting. Just having a game plan to solve the problem and taking action immediately moved me up toward the Empowerment end of the continuum.

Another example of rising above much greater adversity is my husband's ongoing battle with rheumatoid arthritis. He is a dedicated golfer, but the swelling and discomfort associated with the arthritis often deplete his energy, make swinging the golf club a very painful process, and take a tremendous toll on his golf score. He keeps himself on the empowerment side of the line by constantly monitoring his self-talk—what he tells himself about his situation. He makes sure that whether he is playing well or playing poorly, he controls the one thing that he can—the attitude he brings to the game.

Others would probably have given up long ago, but through his persistence and upbeat state of mind, he not only is still playing golf—he and his partner won first place in their flight in a recent tournament.

When you are feeling helpless in an adverse situation, your self-talk is likely to tell you, "There's no way I can make this better." When you are feeling empowered by a strong sense of self-efficacy—your belief in your ability to handle adversity—your self-talk would sound more like that of my husband: "Where there's a will, there's a way!"

Re-Cap: The Components of a Mindset of Hardiness

The Mindset of Hardiness is probably the most powerful component of the Model for Success. It is your mindset that shapes how you respond to adversity, the characteristic that often determines who will succeed and who will fail.

> *"It is your mindset that shapes how you respond to adversity."*

You will remember from Chapter Three that a Mindset of Hardiness has several important components:

- <u>A sense of self-efficacy</u>. The self-efficacy (personal effectiveness) component of your mindset plays a significant role in determining the degree of control you perceive yourself to have over adverse situations. It is your belief in your own ability to handle life's difficulties that provides the motivation that propels you to action.
- <u>An optimistic explanatory style</u>. This is the tendency to expect the best outcome and remain hopeful, even in the most adverse circumstances.
- <u>The 3 C's of Hardiness</u>.
  - √ Control: With a sense of control, people know that they can make choices and influence the events of their lives.
  - √ Challenge: When people enjoy a challenge, stress and adversity are viewed as opportunities to learn and grow.
  - √ Commitment: People who feel committed feel excited about life, involved, and interested, rather than overwhelmed.

- <u>A sense of meaning and purpose</u>. Meaning and purpose provide the "why" in our lives. Living with conscious endeavor provides the "how." A sense of meaning and purpose provides the passion we need to keep striving toward making our vision a reality.

- <u>A clear vision</u>. Our vision is shaped by our sense of meaning and purpose. Our vision becomes our road map; it gives us a sense of direction. Vision enhances commitment to our goals, and allows us to view negative events in our lives as challenges rather than catastrophes.

Each of these components reflects your mindset—beliefs and attitudes that characterize your approach to life's challenges. In Chapter 6, you learned the importance of living with conscious endeavor and with a sense of meaning and purpose as a part of your Mindset of Hardiness. In Chapter 7, you added to your Mindset of Hardiness your vision for your life. The strategies in this chapter will further expand your Mindset of Hardiness and increase your sense of control. They will help you strengthen your self-efficacy, enhance your sense of optimism, develop the 3 C's of stress-hardy people, and provide you with action steps that will empower you to overcome adversity and achieve success.

SEE IT, OWN IT, CHALLENGE IT, FIX IT

This simple but powerful four-step formula will help you strengthen each of the components of the Mindset of Hardiness:

See It

Own It

Challenge It

Fix It

This formula is based on a program developed by researcher Suzanne Oullette and her colleague, Salvadore Maddi. Oullette and Maddi identified responses to stressful situations that characterized stress-hardy people. Then they developed a training program designed to increase resilience to stressful situations. The process they developed, called "situational restructuring," included analyzing the adverse situation, reframing the situation based on real data, and mobilizing oneself to action. Their program strategies form the theoretical basis for the "See It, Own It, Challenge It, Fix It" formula.

As you learn to apply the "See It, Own It, Challenge It, Fix It" formula in your own life, you will become keenly aware of and more accountable for how you typically respond to adversity. As you heighten your accountability, you will develop more confidence in your ability to have an effect on the outcome (increased self-efficacy), and you will become more optimistic about the likelihood of a desirable outcome. You will strengthen your sense of control and notice that you are shifting toward the empowerment end of the Empowerment Continuum. From that position, you are more likely to take action that will have a positive impact on the outcome of difficult situations.

SEE IT

When things don't go our way, many of us still respond in old, subconscious habitual ways that are destructive and dis-empowering. We blame ourselves ("It's all my fault"), or we tell ourselves that our whole life is ruined and there is nothing we can do that will help. We don't usually stop and question our negative automatic thoughts. To make matters worse, our feelings and beliefs about our ability to handle difficult situations often match the negativity of our thoughts. When going for a job interview, if your automatic thought is, "I'll never get that job," and you fuel that thought with feelings of doom, your fear and anxiety can quickly become overwhelming. Your negative thoughts are likely to be reflected in your actions, and often become self-fulfilling prophecies. If you walk into the job interview thinking, "I'll never get this job," you probably won't present yourself with very much confidence, and your chances of getting the job will be greatly reduced.

When something stressful occurs, negative automatic thoughts often quickly pop into our heads uninvited, without reasoning or conscious choice. These negative thoughts are likely to activate a stress response in our bodies, and we may react in ways that are not in our best interests.

In order to empower ourselves to respond more effectively to stress and adversity, we have to identify, interrupt, and change our destructive or self-limiting responses. We start this process by:

- quickly recognizing when adversity strikes, and
- becoming aware of how we typically respond to adversity.

Our goal with *"See It"* is to learn to quickly recognize an adverse event and the negative automatic thoughts or self-talk it produces, along with the effects of that self-talk on our moods and our actions. We can then learn to interrupt the cycle and stop our thoughts from escalating into the debilitating patterns referred to as "awfulizing" and "catastrophizing." When our thoughts are fearful or discouraging, we are less likely to take the constructive action necessary to overcome the challenge and keep persevering toward our goals. As we become more conscious of our negative self-talk and learn to interrupt it, we have the option of choosing a response that will either prevent a potential problem or limit the scope of the problematic situation.

OUR UNIQUE ABILITY

It is the unique ability of human beings to "See It" and to consciously choose how we want to respond to a difficult situation that empowers us. Without this ability things look like this:

Stimulus (Adversity)   Response (Reaction)

When we "See It"—when we quickly recognize adversity and negative self-talk—we have the opportunity to consciously change our self-talk and choose more effective responses. The formula then looks like this:

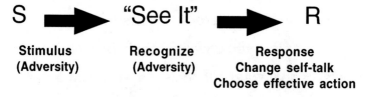

Stimulus   **Recognize**   **Response**
(Adversity)   **(Adversity)**   **Change self-talk**
                                                 Choose effective action

In the situation of the job interview, the interview is being perceived as a stressful event. If you recognize that your automatic thoughts ("I'll never get this job") are creating obstacles on your path to success, you then have the opportunity to interrupt that negativity, and choose a more constructive response such as, "I have a lot of experience and many qualities that make me a good candidate for this job." With this approach, you are more likely to present yourself as a competent, capable person—and to get the job!

When you experience chronic or sustained stress or adversity, you may find that you experience some of the following symptoms:

- **Physical symptoms.** Headaches, indigestion, sleep difficulties, racing heart, and elevated blood pressure
- **Behavioral Symptoms.** Attitude critical of others, inability to get things done, overuse of alcohol, excessive smoking
- **Emotional Symptoms.** Nervousness, anxiety, edginess, feeling powerless to change things, overwhelming sense of pressure, anger, easily upset
- **Cognitive Symptoms.** Trouble thinking clearly, inability to make decisions, constant worry, forgetfulness

Being aware of your body's warning signals is yet another aspect of "See It." Our body usually gives us warning signals, such as those shown above, that help us "See It" and quickly recognize when adversity is occurring. We then are in a position to monitor and change our responses as necessary. Sometimes we cannot recognize the adversity trigger, but if we can identify the symptoms that result, we can become aware of the potential of adversity whenever we experience those symptoms.

It is important to learn to recognize negative automatic thoughts and notice how they affect us physically, behaviorally, emotionally, and cognitively. When our thoughts are fearful or discouraging, over long periods of time we are likely to develop symptoms such as those listed above. We are also less likely to take the constructive action necessary to overcome the challenge and keep persevering toward our goals.

Exercise #1:

The first step in "See It" is to spot the potential adversity. Think of an adverse situation that has recently occurred in your life. Describe it.

_____

_____

Did you quickly see the situation as a potential problem? _____

What triggered your ability to see the situation as a potential problem?

_____

_____

Exercise #2

The next step in "See It" is to identify any negative automatic thoughts that might dis-empower you. Using the adverse situation you identified in Exercise #1, identify your thoughts or self-talk in the situation.

_____

_____

_____

Did your thoughts contribute to feelings of empowerment (feeling of control) or did they increase your feelings of helplessness?

In this next exercise, you are going to rank your thoughts or self-talk based on the Empowerment Continuum shown earlier. Number 1 is a feeling of complete helplessness; 10 is a feeling of total empowerment. The goal of this exercise is to increase your awareness of

- situations that trigger automatic negative reactions, and
- the extent to which your thoughts are destructive and cause you to feel helpless or constructive, giving you a sense of control and empowerment.

When you begin to *"See It,"* you can begin to change the automatic thinking that is limiting or dis-empowering you.

Exercise #3:

In Exercise #1, you identified an adverse situation that you recently experienced. Now identify several other stressful or adverse situations that you have experienced at some time in your life. On a sheet of paper write down your thoughts or self-talk and symptoms from those situations. Using the numbers on the Empowerment Continuum shown earlier, rank your thoughts and self-talk on that scale.

Date	Situation	Thoughts/ Self-Talk	Symptoms experienced	Rating On Scale

Here's an example:

Date: 03-28-02

Situation: My alarm fails to go off.

Your Thoughts: I am going to be late for work. They will think I'm irresponsible. I'll probably lose my job. I can't do anything right.

Symptoms: Physical: racing heart; Cognitive: inability to concentrate.

Rating on Empowerment Scale: 3

What patterns do you see in your self talk?

_____

Which does adversity trigger first for you? (check one) _____Symptoms _____Negative self-talk

What can you do to become aware of the adversity quickly?

My partner Abby shares the following example about an experience her husband Jim had when they were on vacation in New York City. They were waiting in line to go to the top of the Empire State Building. During their wait, Abby noticed that Jim was a little tense. He said he was fine, but as they got on the elevator, Jim's heart started racing and he felt edgy and anxious. By the time they got to the top, Jim realized that the symptoms he was experiencing were an indication that he was experiencing some adversity. When he probed a little deeper he realized that his self-talk said "If you go to the top of the Empire State Building, you might fall off of the roof. You could die." He didn't recognize his fears until the symptoms started. Once he recognized the symptoms and the self-talk, he could change his automatic thinking and incorporate more empowering self-talk such as "I know I can walk the perimeter of the roof safely. The structure is designed for tourists of all ages. My wife is with me and I will be okay." Jim knows that his body is signaling adversity. When he feels edgy, his body is alerting him that there is adversity, and he should pay attention to his self-talk.

Jim recognizes adversity as a result of signals his body gives. Abby, on the other hand, first recognizes adversity when she receives signals in the form of negative self-talk. Her "Critic" barrages her with negativity, a clear signal to Abby that she is experiencing adversity in her life.

Exercise #4:

Now keep track of difficult situations for a week, noting your self-talk, symptoms, and responses. If you need encouragement, find a partner to do this exercise with. Agree with the partner that for the next week, you will give each other a dollar, or put a dollar toward a joint lunch, for every adverse situation you experience and record on the following matrix. See if you can identify fifteen to twenty situations to work with in the exercise below. Then, for each difficult situation, make a note on a sheet of paper identifying your responses (self-talk and/or symptoms) to the difficult situation. Note any patterns.

Date	Situation	Thoughts/ Self-Talk	Symptoms experienced	Rating On Scale

The next step is to rate your responses on the Empowerment Scale. For each response that you rated, ask yourself if your rating places you above the line toward empowerment or below the line toward helplessness. After rating your responses, you will begin to notice whether they have a typical pattern. For example, are your responses usually toward the empowerment end of the continuum or the helplessness end? Do your thoughts often exaggerate or "awfulize" the situation? As you begin to "See It," you will have the opportunity to change any automatic thinking that is limiting or dis-empowering you. When you change your negative thinking, your actions become more constructive.

The Role of Pessimism and Optimism in "See It"

"A pessimist is one who makes difficulties of his opportunities. An optimist is one who makes opportunities of his difficulties."

—Vice-Admiral Mansell, R.N.

Another part of *"Seeing It"* is observing whether your responses to adversity tend to reflect optimism or pessimism. As we know, people who are stress-hardy tend to look at the bright side of situations, and take actions that they believe will improve the outcome of a difficult situation. Pessimists often get stuck in negativity, and often give up quickly when adversity strikes. Look at your responses to the situations listed above in Exercise #4 and ask yourself this question: "Am I exaggerating the problem through negative, pessimistic thinking or am I looking at the problem through the eyes of optimism?"

People who tend to be pessimistic often respond to adversity with what researcher Martin Seligman calls the *3 Ps:*

- Personal. "It's all my fault"
- Pervasive. "I mess up everything I do." (Extend one incident into a general statement), and
- Permanent. "It's the story of my life. Things will never change."

Pessimists tend to think bad events result from personal failings that are unalterable. They "beat themselves up" with self-blame, rather than accepting appropriate blame and learning from the situation.

On the other hand, optimists respond with the attitudes that are characteristic of hardiness. These are known as the 3 Cs:

- Control. "I know I have what it takes to handle this situation."
- Challenge. "This situation is a challenge, not a catastrophe. Where there's a will there is a way."
- Commitment. "I am committed to my goals and will do everything possible to keep moving forward to the achievement of those goals."

Optimists tend to respond to disappointment by formulating a plan and asking others for help. They analyze the situation, accept appropriate blame, challenge and change self-limiting and/or negative thoughts, and take responsibility for achieving the best possible outcome.

Critics of Optimism

During workshops I have presented, I have noticed that participants sometimes become uncomfortable when I suggest that optimism is a key component of a Mindset of Hardiness. They believe that optimism carries with it an implied message that "You don't have to be accountable or take responsibility for the outcome. Just be optimistic and everything will be fine." This is definitely not my message! I tend to be very optimistic, but at the same time, I believe in taking action to achieve the outcomes I want. Our strongest course of action in times of adversity is to maintain an optimistic stance *and* take responsibility for helping to achieve the best possible outcome to the situation, regardless of whose fault the problem is (as we will discuss in "Own It").

Exercise #5:

Because your attitude in times of adversity is critically important to your ability to be successful, it is important to be aware of whether you are typically optimistic or pessimistic. Once you recognize this, you can begin to make changes in your attitude— and research is proving that it is worth the effort! Even small changes in your thinking can profoundly improve your sense of empowerment and ability to cope with adversity.

Ask yourself these questions about your responses to the situations in the previous exercises.

1. "Did I tend to place excessive blame on myself?"
   Yes_____ No_____
2. "Did I have the feeling that the problem extended into other areas of my life?" (I mess up everything I do).
   Yes_____ No_____
3. "Did I see the problem as probably lasting for a very long time, if not forever?"
   Yes_____ No_____
   or
4. "Did I respond with a sense of control, challenge, or commitment?" (Where there's a will, there's a way!)
   Yes_____ No_____

By identifying how you typically respond in difficult situations, you are laying important groundwork for strengthening your response to adversity.

OWN IT

"Own It" means owning the importance of your response to adversity. It means owning your self-talk, owning your actions, and owning the outcome of the situation.

Owning Your Self-Talk

If your self-talk is discouraging, like the statements below, it will create feelings of helplessness and diminish the likelihood that you will take action and achieve your goals. *Some negative self-talk is aimed at our own personal worth:*

> "I'm not good enough."
> "I'll never get it right."
> "I'm not smart enough."

Other negative self-talk is focused on the situation:
> "Because of this situation, I'll probably lose my job."
> "This has ruined my whole life."
> "I'll never find another job I like. "

Recognizing negative beliefs and negative self-talk provides you with the opportunity to challenge and restructure them in a way that will help you feel more optimistic, give you a greater sense of control, and lead you to take more constructive action.

Statements such as these are definitely more empowering!

"I know there is something I can do to improve this situation."

"I'm going to give this my best shot."

"If nothing else, I am going to figure out a way to learn from this situation."

Owning Your Actions

The actions you take in response to adversity are going to determine whether or not you are likely to be successful in achieving your goals. Since your actions are shaped by your self-talk and the feelings generated by that self-talk, the way you respond to life situations looks something like this:

Situation ➡ Self-talk ➡ Response (Feelings and actions)

If your self-talk leans toward the empowering self-talk that is characteristic of optimistic, resilient people, you are likely to feel hopeful and confident, and— most important—to take constructive action.

Example:

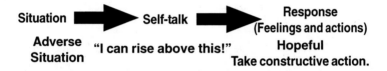

Situation	Self-talk	Response (Feelings and actions)
Adverse Situation	"I can rise above this!"	Hopeful Take constructive action.

If your self-talk leans toward the immobilizing self-talk of the pessimist, you will feel hopeless, discouraged, and will be unlikely to take constructive action.

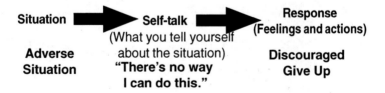

Situation	Self-talk (What you tell yourself about the situation)	Response (Feelings and actions)
Adverse Situation	"There's no way I can do this."	Discouraged Give Up

You are far less likely to take action when you don't believe your actions will improve the outcome of a problematic situation.

Owning the Outcome

In addition to being accountable for your response to difficult situations, "Own It" also means owning the outcome of the situation regardless of who caused the problem. "Owning It" is critical to your ability to achieve success. When you "own it" and hold yourself accountable for doing something to improve the situation, you feel more in control of the situation and are likely to take the necessary action to keep you moving toward your goal.

When I was a member of the team that started "Wellness Link," a behavioral health program that provided a welcome expansion to current hospital services, adversity came in the form of financial problems. While we never expected Wellness Link to be a "money making machine," we did hope that it wouldn't be a financial "white elephant." As the months went by, we began to "See It." We realized that we weren't sustaining the volume of clients necessary to cover our expenses—definitely an adverse situation. Everyone on our team was disappointed and alarmed as the obvious question became, "Should we close our doors and cut the losses?" It was tempting to blame the staff, blame the town for being too small to support a behavioral health center, blame the publicity people for not advertising enough, or blame people in general for not supporting the wonderful services we were providing to the community. I might add that my own negative self-talk wasn't contributing much to the development of a constructive response.

Fortunately, when our team got together to assess this dire situation, we began to realize that it was time to "Own It" by

- taking responsibility for how we were responding to the situation, and
- taking responsibility for the outcome of the situation.

Regardless of why this program was struggling financially, Wellness Link was our dream—a big part of our vision for the hospital—and we were committed to making it work. By owning our responses and taking ownership for the outcome of this adverse situation, we were motivated to take the constructive action that was necessary to start turning things around financially, and we did. While this program continues to have financial challenges, it is still alive and thriving.

Owning and Evaluating Your Response to Adversity

When "owning it" and evaluating your response to adversity, it is important to be able to identify whether your self-talk leans toward an optimistic approach that heightens your sense of control, or a pessimistic approach that discourages you. As yourself the questions:

1. "Do my responses have a customary pattern of optimism or pessimism?"
2. "Do they consistently exaggerate or distort the situation?"
3. "Do I often blame myself unnecessarily?"
4. "Are the actions that I am considering taking reflecting accountability and moving me constructively toward the outcome I desire?"
5. "Am I owning the outcome of this difficult situation?"

When you look at "Own It" from the standpoint of the Empowerment Continuum, it looks like this:

EMPOWERMENT

You "own it" by taking appropriate blame,
learning from mistakes,
and taking the necessary action to achieve the best
possible resolution of the problem situation.

10

9

8

7

6

ADVERSITY

RISE ABOVE IT!

5

4

3

2

1

You view the problem as your fault,
regardless of whether it is;
you beat yourself up, believe that nothing you can do
will make any difference; and you rarely take
responsibility for taking action to achieve
the best possible outcome.

HELPLESSNESS

People who feel empowered are likely to ask themselves what part, if any, they played in creating the problem. The purpose of asking yourself how you might have contributed to the problem is *not* to create dis-empowering blame and self-flagellation. Excessive self-blame is destructive. From a state of mind of excessive self-blame or remorse, you are more likely to doubt yourself, to become discouraged, and even to give up, rather than to learn from the situation and take constructive action. There is a fine line between excessive self-blame and not accepting enough ownership or responsibility for the outcome of a situation. When we accept no ownership for the problem, we run the risk of accepting no responsibility for achieving the best possible outcome or resolution to the problem—a very dis-empowering stance! The ideal response is to examine the problem, accept an appropriate level of blame for any role you may have played in creating the problem, learn from the experience, and take appropriate action to resolve the problem.

Thus, the purpose of "Own It" is to strengthen your sense of control by:

✓ taking responsibility for your self-talk and your actions in response to the adversity (recognizing that negative self-talk gets in the way of your ability to achieve your goals), and

✓ assuming ownership for achieving the best possible outcome of the situation.

Exercise #6:

Within the next week, notice when a stressful or adverse situation occurs. Ask yourself these empowering questions to help you "Own It":

1. What is the problem?
2. What is my self-talk about this situation? Is it empowering or discouraging?
3. What portion of the problem is actually my fault?
4. What can I learn from this situation? How can I see this as a challenge from which to grow?
5. To what extent am I willing to take responsibility for improving the outcome?

The key is to make sure that your self-talk in adverse situations is near the empowerment end of the continuum. If not, it is time to challenge your self-talk and fix it, as we will learn in the next two steps of our formula!

Exercise #7:

Every day for the next two weeks, list six to ten answers that express a response to each of the sentence completion exercises listed below. Do them quickly, just a few minutes each. Write down the answers as fast as you can. Don't stop to think about an answer, don't worry about if it's correct, true, realistic, significant—just write.

Note: In his book, *Taking Responsibility,* Nathaniel Branden notes that the key to effective sentence completion exercises is to stay focused on completing the stems in rapid succession, and avoid censoring anything you write. Don't set any expectations of what might happen, should happen. Just go with the flow. Don't read what you wrote the day before as you sit down to write each day. At the end of each week, reflect upon your endings and insights.

Stem questions:

If I am conscious of my response to adversity I experience, then:

1. _____

2. _____

3. _____

4. _____

5. _____

6. _____

If I operate semi-consciously and don't acknowledge my self-talk around adverse events/situations, then:

1. _____

2. _____

3. _____

4. _____

5. _____

6. _____

The bad thing about acknowledging my self-talk around adverse events/situations is:

_____

_____

If I take responsibility for my self-talk, then:

_____

_____

CHALLENGE IT

"Challenge It" means that, once you recognize pessimistic, destructive self-talk and beliefs about yourself or your situation, you take steps to challenge and/or dispute them. Most of us have automatic thoughts and reactions to negative situations that are programmed into our system at a very deep level. We often barely notice our automatic responses even though they may be quite self-limiting and extremely dis-empowering. In the Wellness Link situation, I was hardly aware of the undercurrent of old beliefs and negative self-talk that was telling me that I didn't have what it took to make that program a success and that I was probably in over my head.

What is needed is bring negative responses to a conscious level. When we are conscious of negative thoughts, we can challenge them and limit their debilitating effects, and ultimately choose more constructive responses that focus on the problem at hand.

You begin to "Challenge It" by asking:

1. Am I responding to this problem with pessimistic, negative beliefs and self-talk that might be limiting my ability to take constructive action in this situation?
2. Am I jumping to conclusions?
3. What evidence is there to support my negative beliefs and self-talk?
4. How much of what I am telling myself is based in reality?
5. Am I "catastrophizing?"
6. How can I look at this situation in a more constructive way?
7. What's the worst thing that could happen? Can I handle it?

Exercise #8

Using the stressful or adverse situation you identified in Exercise #4, ask yourself these questions to help you challenge any negative self-talk you might have:

1. Am I responding to this problem with pessimistic, negative beliefs and self-talk that might be limiting my ability to take constructive action in this situation?
2. Am I jumping to conclusions?
3. What evidence is there to support my negative beliefs and self-talk.
4. How much of what I am telling myself is based in reality?
5. Am I "catastrophizing?"
6. How can I look at this situation in a more constructive way?
7. What's the worst thing that could happen? Can I handle it?

Exercise #9:

(Use the format shown at the end of this exercise to complete these activities).

1. **Negative Self-talk**: Identify your destructive thought. Example: I blew that interview. I am never going to get a job!
2. **Rational Support:** Ask yourself how much rational support there is for that self talk. Example: Not very much, there are thousands of jobs. I am sure I can find one of them.

3. **Challenge it**: Identify the evidence for the true and the untrue portions of this self talk, thought or belief and why:

    a. True portion: Example: I didn't do as well on the interview as I hoped.

    b. Untrue portion: Example: I blew it. I am never going to get a job. Why? Because: I don't know that I blew the interview. This is only one job interview in the entire world. Even if I did blow it, it doesn't mean I am never going to get a job!

4. **Worst thing that could happen:** Define the worst thing that could happen to me in this situation. Example, I might not get this job and the interviewer might think I was not worthy of the responsibility or salary this job offers.

5. **Learn from it**: Ask yourself what you can learn from this situation. Example: I need to sharpen my interview skills.

6. **Reframe**: Substitute more constructive self-talk. This reframe must be believable. If you don't believe it, it won't move you toward empowerment. Example: I am disappointed I did

235

not perform well in this interview. I can practice my interview skills and will do better on the next one.

Negative Self-talk	Rational Support: The evidence that this thought is true	Challenge it: The evidence that this thought is not true (Irrational support)	Worst thing that could happen	Learn from it	Reframe

Look at your list of negative self-talk above. How many of the destructive self-talks would you ever say to a friend if you were evaluating their behavior toward a situation or event? Most people would never talk in such a way to a friend, so why should we talk to ourselves that way?

Exercise #10:

Using the list of negative self-talk above, define the words you are using to describe yourself.

Do those words really fit you?

_____

People who call themselves idiots, jerks, etc. will see that when they define it, it usually does not fit for them. It is not accurate for who they are. Use the process above to reframe.

Exercise #11:

If you are having a difficult time reframing your negative thought, you may be receiving some intrinsic value from your attachment to that negative thought. For example, your negative self-talk is that you are incompetent and employers see that and don't offer you a job. This self-talk may be providing you a payoff. For example, by seeing yourself as incompetent and unable to get a job, you get to be taken care of by your spouse and get attention from other family members and friends. You may see that negative self-talk as providing you with the opportunity to stay a victim. That may be enough of a payoff to keep you from changing. If you think that may be the case, you may find this next exercise helpful in doing a cost/benefit analysis of your negative self-talk:

Thought:	Payoff:	Cost:
Negative/destructive self-talk/thought	How this negative self-talk helps me/payoff	How this negative self-talk hurts me/cost

FIX IT

After you have asked yourself the "Challenge It' questions, you will want to determine at what point you are ready to take action. Remember, the goal is to regain a sense of control and to overcome the deepest fears of the pessimist:

- It's all my fault.
- This might extend into my whole life.
- Things will never change.

"Fix It" is the action step that allows you to overcome adversity and achieve success. Being willing to take action to make a situation better reflects high ownership and high accountability. It empowers you by heightening your sense of control over the situation. When the problem or difficult situation is caused by someone else, it is tempting to say, "It's not my fault. I had nothing to do with this situation"— and then wash your hands of the problem. But in doing that, you give up any control you might have over how much damage occurs as a result of the problem, and whether you are able to keep moving toward your goals in spite of the adversity.

> *"You strengthen your sense of control when you make a commitment to "Fix It" by taking appropriate constructive action."*

You strengthen your sense of control when you make a commitment to "Fix It" by taking appropriate constructive action.

Exercise #12:

Ask yourself these questions to help determine what action you wish to take:

1. What can I do to gain more control over the situation?

_____

_____

2. What parts of the problem must I acknowledge as my fault? (You probably did this in "Own It").

_____

_____

3. How broad must this problem be in my life?

_____

_____

4. What can I do to limit the scope of the problem in my life?

_____

_____

5. What can I do to minimize the length of time this problem will last?

_____

_____

6. What actions can I take to achieve the best possible outcome to this difficult situation and keep me moving toward my goals?

_____

_____

The answers to these questions will empower you and prepare you to take the following action steps:

1. Objectively evaluate the real root cause(s) of the problem at hand.

_____

_____

2. Make a list of possible solutions/actions to address the root cause(s).

_____

_____

3. List the pro's and con's of the possible solutions/ actions and the possible consequences that you should plan for.

_____

_____

4. Evaluate each possible action against how well it will improve the outcome and how much risk/effort/ cost/time it will take to implement.

_____

_____

5. Select and implement the action that gives the best results for the least risk/effort/cost/time.

_____

_____

6. Rate yourself on the empowerment scale now as compared to when the adverse situation or event first occurred.

_____

_____

By asking yourself these questions and taking the action steps, you will empower yourself to **RISE ABOVE IT,** achieve the best possible outcome to adverse events, and continue moving toward making your vision for your life a reality.

• •

Continuously Acquire Life Skills For Effectiveness 9

As you go through your life, it is important to continually increase your ability to respond effectively to life's difficulties. By strengthening and developing your repertoire of life skills, you dramatically enhance your ability to rise above adversity, and to consistently move toward the success you want in your life.

As we discussed in Chapter Four, key life skills help you build a strong personal foundation of empowerment. Some of these key life skills that will help you respond more effectively to stressful situations and adversity are:

- Eliciting the Body's Relaxation Response on a Regular Basis
- Reframing Your Perspective on Challenging Situations
- Communicating Effectively
- Renewing Your Energy
- Managing Your Time

- Maintaining a Sense of Humor
- Managing Your Finances
- Networking Effectively

ELICITING THE BODY'S RELAXATION RESPONSE

We know that chronic stress is harmful to our health and sense of well-being. It is essential to learn skills and to implement strategies that will help you control and neutralize these effects.

The greatest teachers in many religious traditions have long valued the importance of a quiet mind. It is believed that a quiet mind is what allows us to best connect with our own inner wisdom. More recently, researchers have found that quieting our minds allows us to elicit the relaxation response in our bodies. Studies have shown that when we are able to quiet our minds for as little as fifteen to twenty minutes a day, positive physiological effects occur in our bodies. These effects include a decreased heart rate and lowered blood pressure, which helps us counteract the negative effects of daily stress that result in health problems such as strokes and heart attacks.

As a person who has struggled with high blood pressure, I can personally attest to the value of consciously quieting your mind and relaxing your body. I was placed on blood pressure medication shortly before learning how to elicit the relaxation response. As I began to do some of the exercises in this chapter, I was able to discontinue the medication (under the supervision of a physician) and maintain healthy blood pressure levels. But decreased blood pressure wasn't my only benefit. As I learned to relax, I felt much lighter in spirit and life was joyous rather than burdensome!

In order to achieve the beneficial results of the relaxation response, you may need to choose techniques that help you relax and "let go" more easily. Relaxing and letting go physically involves releasing muscles from habitual tension, breathing slowly and regularly, and using the exhalation of your breath to release tension. Letting go emotionally means cultivating an attitude of calmness and composure. Mentally letting go means observing and releasing troubling, worrisome thoughts. You give yourself a great gift by letting go and eliciting the relaxation response on a daily basis. While you can't always do away with the stress in your life, you can allow yourself to relax and renew by quieting your mind. In doing this, you relieve tension and anxiety, and allow your body to start the healing process.

Deep belly breathing is a great stress management tool and a skill that is helpful when eliciting the relaxation response. Many of us aren't aware of the important role that the breath plays in relaxation. When you breathe in, you provide your body with oxygen, which is used to produce energy. When you breathe out, you release the carbon dioxide which is produced in this process. People have two ways of breathing: thoracic breathing (chest breathing) and diaphragmatic breathing (also known as abdominal or deep belly breathing.). Sometimes breathing is a combination of both. Diaphragmatic breathing is best when you are practicing eliciting the relaxation response. When you do deep belly breathing, you begin to feel some control over anxiety and tension. Exercise 3 below uses diaphragmatic breathing.

Methods for Eliciting the Relaxation Response

There are many ways to elicit the relaxation response. Some common methods are:

- Meditation
- Diaphragmatic Breathing
- Imagery
- Mindfulness
- Progressive Muscle Relaxation
- Yoga Stretching

Although each of these techniques seem different, all of them have two basic components:

- The use of a focusing device such as repeating a word or phrase, and
- The adoption of a passive attitude toward thoughts that are distracting. If your thoughts distract you, gently direct your mind back to your focus device.

General Instructions for Eliciting the Relaxation Response

1. Find a comfortable place to sit.
2. Make a habit of using the same location each day. In doing this, you will find that you will start to

relax by simply being there. Make sure that you won't be disturbed and that your telephone is un-plugged.

3. Close your eyes.
4. Relax your muscles.
5. Breath slowly and repeat your focus word on the exhale.
6. It is a good idea to elicit the relaxation response at the same time(s) each day. This helps make it a habit.
7. If your thoughts wander, gently bring them back to your focus.
8. It is advisable to elicit the relaxation response at least once a day for fifteen to twenty minutes. I've heard it said that the only bad relaxation session is one that's not done—and I agree.

The bottom line is that we are happier, calmer, more effective, and more fulfilled than when we begin to cultivate a quiet mind and elicit the body's relaxation response.

Exercise #1: Quiet Your Mind

During the coming week, start to pay attention to your mind. At the times that you begin to feel tense, observe your thoughts: Are they racing? Are you feeling uncomfortable feelings such as fear and anxiety? Try to count the number of times each day that your busy mind and racing thoughts cause you significant feelings of discomfort. (Later exercises will teach you how to relax your mind when you are feeling tense.) Using the following scale, record how frequently you feel discomfort on any given day because of a busy mind and racing thoughts.

Never	Sometimes	Often	Very Often	Almost Always

Never =1, Sometimes = 2, Often = 3, Very Often = 4, Almost Always = 5

Exercise #2: "Respiratory One"

Meditation is one of the techniques used to elicit the relaxation response. Meditation is the process of focusing the mind on an object or activity (such as your breathing.) As you practice meditation, your body and your mind will begin to quiet down, and you will notice that you are experiencing a state of physiological and mental rest.

Try this "Respiratory One" meditation technique developed by Herbert Benson, M.D., Associate Professor of Medicine at the Mind/Body Medical Institute of Harvard Medical School.

1. Sit quietly in a comfortable position with your eyes closed.

2. Deeply relax all your muscles. It sometimes helps
    to tense and then release them starting with your
    feet and legs and working upward.
3. Breathe deeply through your nose and be aware
    of your breath.
4. Say the word "one" silently while exhaling.

Note: Dr. Benson suggests that you use the word
"one" for every breath, rather than trying to count
your breaths, losing track, and becoming stressed.

Exercise #3: The "Mini"

Most of us experience a stressful event during the
course of a day. When this occurs, the following
mini-relaxation exercise can be helpful in regaining
your calm. When you do a "mini," you will probably
find that you feel remarkable refreshed, better able
to concentrate, and even able to more easily relate
with others. Here are the instructions for doing a
"mini":

1. Put your right hand just under your navel (belly
    button).
2. Breathe in through your nose and out through
    your mouth.
3. Focus on breathing down into your stomach, not
    just into your chest.

4. Allow your hand to rise as you breathe in and to fall as you breathe out.

5. As you inhale, say the number "ten" to yourself. Exhale.

6. With the next breath, say the number "nine", then breathe out.

7. Do this until you reach zero.

Exercise #4: Guided Imagery

Guided imagery is another enjoyable method for eliciting the relaxation response. There are many guided imagery tapes available. One of these is my own tape, "Relax and Renew," in which I take the listener for a delightful imaginary walk on a beach. This tape is available through my website, *www.donnadaisy.com*. You might try guided imagery by first borrowing a guided imagery tape from a friend. You might also try just visualizing a peaceful walk in the woods, or resting comfortably by a calm, beautiful lake, and noticing all of the delightful sights, sounds, and fragrances of nature.

Exercise #5: Hatha Yoga/Gentle Stretching

Hatha yoga, or gentle stretching exercises can also be a pleasant way to elicit the relaxation response and calm the mind. I find it helpful to use a tape, as in guided imagery, and follow the instructions as I move from one stretch to the next. Many excellent tapes are available. My tape, *Stretch and Renew*, guides you through exercises to release muscle tension and is available on my website, *www.donnadaisy.com.*

Exercise #6: Progressive Muscle Relaxation and Diaphragmatic Breathing

1. Start this exercise in a sitting position, becoming aware of your breathing. Breathe deeply into your belly. Notice that your belly expands when you breathe in and flattens when you breathe out. Notice the natural movements of breath and body, and concentrate on feelings. Do this diaphragmatic breathing for about a minute.

2. Next, become aware of your feet. Inhale to the count of ten, stretching your toes back toward your body. Feel the tightness in your calves. Hold your breath for ten counts, and exhale, relaxing the muscles to the count of twenty (or whatever is comfortable.) Your exhale will be somewhat longer than the "in" breath. Now notice the feelings of relaxation in your calves and feet while you continue to breathenaturally(without counting to twenty.)

3. Repeat the pattern of bringing your awareness to each body part, and tensing, holding, and relaxing with your breathing for the following areas:

- Buttocks and perineum: Tighten on the inhale, relax on the exhale.
- Belly: Tighten on the inhale, relax on the exhale.
- Chest: Tighten on the inhale, relax on the exhale.
- Shoulders: Lift them to your ears as you inhale, lower as you exhale.
- Arms and Hands: Flex your wrists back toward your body as you inhale, relax them as you exhale.
- Face: Scowl, puckering your face like a raisin on the inhale, relax your face on the exhale.
- Relax your neck by slowly moving your head from side to side while continuing to focus on your breathing.

REFRAMING YOUR PERSPECTIVE ON CHALLENGING SITUATIONS

You may not be able to change your situation, but you can change your mental frame of reference. A key life skill in maintaining a sense of control and a perspective of optimism is reframing or situational restructuring. While the concept of reframing is covered in the chapters

> *"You may not be able to change your situation, but you can change your mental frame of reference."*

on Mindset of Hardiness, the ability to reframe adverse situations is definitely an important life skill.

Reframing simply means looking at an event from a different perspective. One of the best examples of different perspectives is looking at a glass that is filled halfway with water. Do you see it as half full or half empty? An example of a beautiful reframe is this response by an individual describing a failed project: "I'm not a failure if I don't succeed. I'm a success because I tried."

By looking at the situation from this positive and encouraging perspective, this person avoided feeling defeated, and was able to rethink the project and look for possible new solutions. Every day we have a choice about the way we choose to see things—our frame of reference. Is a traffic jam an annoying, blood-pressure-raising event, or do you see it as an opportunity to relax and listen to that new CD? Is a busy day a cause for stress and frustration, or evidence that your business is quite successful? Having the ability to look at things from a different perspective is a great tool when building the strong personal foundation that allows you to rise above adversity. One of the great masters of the art of reframe, Joan Borysenko, tells a wonderful story that beautifully illustrates the power of reframe. She describes a church in Southern California whose minister was so wise and charismatic that each Sunday the church was filled and overflowing. During one of the services, there was a shortage of chairs, and the ushers were trying to find a spot for those not yet seated. As the congregation began to get restless, one of the ushers approached a microphone and made this announcement: "Isn't it wonderful that so many people turned out this morning? If you're disturbed about starting a few minutes late, we cordially invite you to change your mind." The crowd chuckled and began to relax as they set aside their irritation and thought about how nice it was that so many people had chosen to come to their church.

If you tend to be a pessimist, reframing problems that occur in your life is a skill that you definitely want to add to your "bag of tricks."

Exercise #7:
Start by noticing some problems that are causing you to feel stressed, worried, upset, etc. Ask yourself how you might be able to reframe the problems so that you can see a lighter, brighter side to them and view

the problems as challenges to be overcome rather than as catastrophies.

Problem:

What was your distressing thought?

_____

_____

What is another way to look at that problem (a possible reframe)?

_____

_____

Use this technique frequently whenever a problem or situation feels overwhelming and discouraging. Thinking of it as a challenge can be a great energizer!

Exercise #8:

Another way to reframe is to notice when you find yourself judging, complaining, or feeling upset about a problem or situation. Challenge yourself to put yourself in the other person's shoes and reframe the situation by identifying at least two good reasons *why* they might have behaved that way. For example, say I am reviewing my big project with my boss and he snaps at me. He points out all the flaws in my work and criticizes my performance. I could reframe the situation by recognizing that he is criticizing me because he is under tremendous pressure by his boss on this project and he is depending on me to do a good job because this project is outside of his area of expertise. Or I could reframe by recognizing that his style is to keep me on my toes by criticizing me. While that style is ineffective for me, recognizing that it works for him can free me up to focus on doing a good job on the project and not become overwhelmed by the criticism.

COMMUNICATING EFFECTIVELY

Effective communication is a key skill that is essential to your ability to rise above adversity and skillfully handle difficult situations. Assertive communication allows you to consider your alternatives and speak from a place of wisdom. Remember, the three keys to effective communication are:

- You act out of awareness and choice.
- You express your feelings openly, honestly, and appropriately.

- You encourage the other person to express his or her feelings.

Effective communication includes being able to express your likes and dislikes, knowing how to accept a compliment, and knowing when to say "yes" and when to say "no". In Chapter Four, we discussed communication styles including assertive communication, aggressive communication, passive-aggressive communication, and passive communication. In their book, The Wellness Book, Dr. Herbert Benson and Eileen Stuart suggest some communication techniques which I have found helpful in dealing with some of the most common communication problems.

One technique is to simply say "thank you" when receiving a complement rather than minimizing the compliment by saying something like "It was nothing." Another great technique is looking for the win-win solution. As suggested by Stephen Covey in his book, The 7 Habits of Highly Effective People, seeking solutions that are mutually beneficial is a helpful approach when trying to work out a difference of opinion. This is a far more effective approach than trying to prove you are right and the other person is wrong.

A critical strategy for effective communication is to say what you need and be specific. It is easy to fall into expecting people to read your mind. Instead, ask for what you need in very specific terms.

Still another great technique is to know when to say "yes" and when to say "no." Many of us have trouble saying no when asked to take on a task or to do something for somebody. We are afraid the person will be angry with us or will feel rejected. It is important to be clear that you are saying "no" to the task and not the person. For example, you might say, "I really appreciate your thinking of me, but I can't commit to that right now." (Learning to say "no" will be discussed further in the Energy Renewal section.)

Other great strategies for effective communication include actively listening and acknowledging what the other person says, showing empathy and demonstrating an understanding of where the other person is coming from, and paying attention to body language.

A strategy that improves the effectiveness of your communication in any relationship is the use of "I" messages. When you have a concern that you want to address with someone, the following are some good general guidelines.

- Start with the word "I",
- Be direct,
- Be immediate,
- Be specific,
- Be honest, and
- Be sensitive to the occasions and the people involved.

The following is a general format for assertive communication with the use of "I" messages. Be sure to see the example below to help you understand how to effectively use this formula:

I feel _____ (you put in the feeling such as sad, angry, scared, etc.) *when you* _____ (fill in the behavior) *because* _____(fill in the explanation. Explain how you honestly see the situation.) *I need you to*_____
(describe what you are asking the person to change.)

Example: "I feel sad and angry when you are late for dinner, because I value the time we have together. I need you to start getting home sooner."

The following are exercises that will provide you an opportunity to practice specific communication styles and strategies.

Exercise #9:
Most of us have moments when it is difficult to express ourselves well, to disagree with someone, or to comfortably say "no." Identify some specific situations in which you have trouble expressing yourself openly, honestly, and appropriately.

Are there people with whom you have trouble expressing yourself openly and honestly? If so, identify them here.

_____

_____

Exercise #10:
We all have areas of strength and weakness in our communication skills. Rate yourself on how effective you are in each of these important communication components.

261

Saying "Thank you."

1   2   3   4   5   6   7   8   9   10
Not very effective   Very effective

Looking for win-win situations:

1   2   3   4   5   6   7   8   9   10
Not very effective   Very effective

Say what I mean:

1   2   3   4   5   6   7   8   9   10
Not very effective   Very effective

Be specific:

1   2   3   4   5   6   7   8   9   10
Not very effective   Very effective

Know when to say "Yes"

1   2   3   4   5   6   7   8   9   10
Not very effective   Very effective

Know when to say "No" and do it effectively!

1   2   3   4   5   6   7   8   9   10
Not very effective   Very effective

Active Listening:

1   2   3   4   5   6   7   8   9   10
Not very effective   Very effective

Empathy:

1   2   3   4   5   6   7   8   9   10
Not very effective   Very effective

Knowing my body language:

1   2   3   4   5   6   7   8   9   10
Not very effective   Very effective

Congratulations on the things you scored high on! The next couple of exercises will help you work on those aspects that need improvement. And don't worry if you didn't score high on very many. You've taken a very important first step in raising your communication skills.

Exercise #11: Identifying Communication Styles

One of the best ways to improve the quality of your current relationships is by practicing assertive communication.   The following situations are ones in which many of us find ourselves. They are aggravating or upsetting, and they can easily cause us to act in an unhealthy, aggressive, or passive manner. We don't have to merely react as we might have done in the past. Instead, we can consciously choose to communicate effectively. Each situation has four response spaces after it. For each situation, write out how you would respond in an aggressive way, in a passive-aggressive way, a passive way, and in an assertive way. There are some blanks for you to think of your own stressful situation. This will give you a chance to practice finding assertive responses in areas relevant to your unique life. Here's an example: You're at work, and your boss asks you to take on another project you just don't have time for.

Aggressive: "What are you thinking? I'm so busy right now I don't have time to use the restroom when I need to, let alone take on another project!"

Passive-Aggressive: "Well, let me think. I'm just not sure right now." (Like I have time for this!) "Can I get back to you tomorrow?" (I'll forget you even asked about this as soon as you leave.)

Passive: "Well, I guess I can. I don't know how I'm going to get it done, but I'm sure your project is more important than anything else I'm working on. I'll just have to work through all my lunch hours and stay late."

Assertive: "I respect your need to get this project completed, but I am already working on several projects. If you could wait a week, I'd have plenty of time to work on it. Right now, though, my work load would not allow me to give my best effort to your project."

Situation: A co-worker always takes the last cup of coffee—and never makes more.

Aggressive: ———————————————

Passive-Aggressive: ————————————

Passive: —————————————————

Assertive: ——————————————————

Situation: Your best friend cancels the lunch date you've been looking forward to for a week.

Aggressive: ———————————————

Passive-Aggressive: ————————————

Passive: —————————————————

Assertive: ——————————————————

Situation: Your son/daughter deliberately disobeys you and goes out with friends while grounded.

Aggressive: ———————————————

Passive-Aggressive: ————————————

Passive: —————————————————

Assertive: ——————————————————

Situation: Your spouse/significant other failed to do (insert task of choice here) again!

Aggressive: ———————————————

Passive-Aggressive: ————————————

Passive: —————————————————

Assertive: ——————————————————

Situation: You take your car to the shop to get it fixed. When you get it back, the problem's still there, but they charged you anyway.

Aggressive: _____

Passive-Aggressive: _____

Passive: _____

Assertive: _____

Situation of your choice:

Aggressive: _____

Passive-Aggressive: _____

Passive: _____

Assertive: _____

Situation of your choice:

Aggressive: _____

Passive-Aggressive: _____

Passive: _____

Assertive: _____

Exercise #12: Using "I" Statements

At those times when we want to address a specific issue with someone (anger, dissatisfaction) and wish to ask that person to do something differently, it is important not to choose words that are critical and judgmental ("You're always late! Why can't you ever be on time?") Such words create defensiveness and barriers to communication. Try, instead, communicating your feelings and expressing your needs by using "I" statements ("When you are late, I feel discounted and disrespected"), explain why you feel the way you do (because I really value our time together), and ask for what you need ("I need you to be on time.") The person will feel less defensive and be more open to hear what you have to say. The following assertiveness formula can be helpful:

1. Identify the situation you would like changed.
2. Identify your feeling.
3. State why you feel the way you do.
4. State what you want/need the person to do differently.

Example:
1. Identify the situation you would want to change: "When you are late"
2. Identify the feeling " . . . I feel discounted and disrespected."
3. State why: " . . because I really value our time together."
4. State what you want/need the person to do differently.

Exercise #13:

Think of some situations in your own life where you feel the need to express dissatisfaction and/or ask for change. These situations may be with family members, friends, co-workers, or other people. Try using the above formula to express yourself assertively using "I" statements.

Situation:

1. Identify the situation and the person:

_____

2. Identify your feeling:

_____

3. State why:

_____

4. Ask for what you need:

_____

Situation:

1. Identify the situation and the person:

_____

2. Identify your feeling:

_____

3. State why:

_____

4. Ask for what you need:

_____

Situation:

1. Identify the situation and the person:

_____

2. Identify your feeling:

_____

3. State why:

_____

4. Ask for what you need:

_____

Practice this formula the next time you wish to express dissatisfaction or ask for change. You might be pleasantly surprised by how effective this kind of interaction can be when you are making a request to get your needs met.

Set Boundaries

One form of assertive communication is setting boundaries. Boundaries are the guidelines or rules that you set for how others may treat you. Boundaries define what others may say to you and what others are allowed to do to you. As I mentioned in Chapter Four, setting boundaries is a must for maintaining a sense of control over your life.

So often we put up with disrespectful, demeaning behaviors from others because we have never learned
that we have the right to tell another person that their
painful words or actions are not okay. The following
exercise will help you start to identify those with whom
you need to set boundaries, and provide you with an
opportunity   to   practice   assertively
setting boundaries.

Exercise #14:

Take a moment to identify some occasions when a
person was physically or verbally hurtful.   Then
identify what that person said or did that hurt your
feelings or caused you to feel bad about yourself.
The final step is to practice how you will
assertively tell that person that it is not all right to
treat you in that way.

Example: "When you yell at me, I feel devalued
and unloved. I need you to talk to me in a calm
way that allows us to work constructively toward
a solution to this problem."

Occasion: _____

Person: _____

What that person said or did that was hurtful:

_____

Assertive statement setting boundaries:

_____

Don't forget: When people refuse to honor the boundaries you set, you may choose to detach and end an unhealthy relationship!

RENEWING YOUR ENERGY

Last winter when visiting my daughter, Kathy, in Atlanta, she took my hand and said, "Mom, you don't seem to have the enthusiasm and the energy that you usually have. Is anything wrong?" My first reactive response was "Nothing is wrong. I'm fine." But Kathy's observation hit me like a 2 x 4. I knew that my life had become terribly out of balance—all work and no play. I was neglecting friends and family members, was letting my physical appearance slide, and wasn't even exercising very much. My self-talk went something like this: "Oh well, I'm getting old. These things don't matter much anymore."

Needless to say, I was doing next to nothing to replenish my energy reserves. It was as if I had forgotten everything I ever knew about taking care of myself.

I had fallen into some pretty poor self-care (or lack of self-care) habits, and was grateful for the support and love of my family and the wise counsel of many good friends. After the conversation with Kathy, I quickly began to re-prioritize how I was spending my time. I made an appointment to get my hair styled, and began re-instituting my exercise program. My new puppy, Abby, made it easy to start building both fun and exercise back into my daily routine since she practically "begged" to take long walks, and loved to romp and play as we went along.

The results were instantaneous and pretty amazing. My enthusiasm for both work and play returned, and my husband couldn't believe the difference in my appearance. He said that I looked like I did in college. (I'll have to go back to my college yearbook to make sure that is a compliment!)

Think back to the analogy of the beautiful golden cup filled with your life energy. Just as I had allowed my life energy to be drained without refilling it, each of you has things that drain the energy from your golden cup. But we also have things that refill that cup with energy. The goal is always be aware of the level of your energy, and keep refilling your cup as the energy supply gets low.

Exercise #15:

One way to constantly tune in to your energy supply is to create an "energy rating scale" with numbers from 1 to 10. One represents empty. Ten represents full.

```
ENERGY RATING SCALE
     10 - FULL
         9
         8
         7
         6
         5
         4
         3
         2
     1 - EMPTY
```

Draw a circle around the number that represents your energy level right now. Learn to recognize where the cut-off point is for feeling good and functioning at full capacity. This "energy level scale" is a great tool for staying aware of your personal resources, and keeping your energy renewed. By honestly assessing and tracking your energy level two or three times a day, over time you can begin refueling your energy as soon as you notice that you are "running on low." The magic number for me is 7. If my energy level ranking is much below that, I know I am on dangerous ground and better make some changes - - quickly!

What Drains Our Energy?

It is important to become aware of things that drain our energy. Some typical energy drains are worry, resentments, unfinished business, clutter in our lives, information over-load, certain people-and the list goes on and on.

Exercise #16:

The following is a checklist of common energy drains. Read the list and check the things that are draining the energy from your cup. Once you have identified your energy drains, you can prioritize the ones you need to eliminate from your life and start getting rid of them!

Personal Life:

____ I have relationships in my life that drain my energy rather than replenish it.

____ I have very few family members or close friends with whom I can share concerns.

____ I am harboring resentments toward people in my life.

____ I don't take time to nurture friendships.

____ I have issues with family members that need to be resolved.

____ Other:

____ Other:

Professional Life:

____ I have a job that I don't enjoy.

____ I have conflicts with co-workers that drain my energy.

____ I seem always to have more work than I can deal with.

____ I'm frustrated because I receive more E mails, faxes, etc. than I can deal with.

____ I don't have the skills I need to do my job.

____Other: _____

____Other: _____

Environment:

____My closet is so jammed that I have trouble finding what I need.

____My desk is so cluttered that just looking at it overwhelms me.

____The lighting in my reading area is poor.

____I have a lot of things that need repairing (car, appliances, fences).

____My work and/or home environment isn't very cheerful.

____Other: _____

____Other: _____

By checking the items that apply to your life, you can begin to get an idea of what drains your energy and start making plans to eliminate this energy drain. One of the best books available on identifying energy drains is *Take Time for Your Life* by Cheryl Richardson. I would encourage you to add a copy of that book to your reading list for life skills and self-care.

Refilling Your Cup

Now that you have started eliminating energy drains from your life, you will want to start thinking about things that will help refill your golden cup with energy. Your objective is always to know how full your cup is, and to keep doing the things that you know will rejuvenate your energy. The types of things you can do to refill your cup basically fall into two categories: Those you can do immediately, and long-term strategies. You will find many long-term strategies for keeping your cup refilled in Chapter Five, Lifestyle of Self-Care. Some short-term strategies that people find helpful are:

- Taking a walk.
- Getting rid of clutter (cleaning out a closet, organizing your desk, etc.)
- Reading a few pages of a good book.
- Doing a "mini" relaxation exercise.
- Including 15 to 30 minutes of physical exercise in your daily routine.
- Starting the day with 10 to 15 minutes of meditation or "quieting your mind."
- Getting some fresh flowers to beautify your work or living environment.
- Eating healthier foods and less junk food.

- Spending time with a family member or friend with whom you feel close.
- Maintaining a network of friends you can turn to in times of need.

Start keeping track of your energy reserves by using your Energy Rating scale frequently. Checking at least two to three times daily is a good idea. If you find that your energy reserves are low, take action immediately to refill your cup. In addition to your short term activities, be sure that you are incorporating into your life long-term self-care strategies such as regular exercise and healthy diet as well.

Learn to Say "No"

Jennifer White, author of the book *Work Less, Make More*, made the observation that saying yes to yourself (your own self-care) may mean having to say no to something—or someone—else. Learning to say "no" with grace and ease is a life skill that will play a big role in avoiding energy drains and reducing stress.

This is where your effective communication skills come in handy. If you are like most of us, you probably say yes to a lot of things that really aren't among your priorities. For example, you agree to go to lunch with someone because she has asked you several times and you feel obligated, or you take on extra projects at work despite the fact that your plate is already too full.

Saying no can be difficult, but it becomes easier when you have given some thought to how you are going to say "no". Here are some tips for saying "no" effectively:

- Stick with the truth,
- Be direct, and
- Be gracious.

In her book, Jennifer White makes several suggestions for assertively saying "no." The first is to simply say, "Thanks, but I'll have to pass on that." No further explanation is necessary. Another approach is the "gracious no," in which you assertively express yourself by saying something like, "I appreciate you thinking of me, but my time is already committed." The thing I like most about that approach is that you are telling the truth. Even if your time isn't already committed to another person or task, it is committed to taking care of yourself.

Another assertive way of saying "no" is the "my family is the reason" no. Each day, I have special blocks of time reserved for my husband. That commitment is important to both of us. Too often in the past, I have told my husband that I couldn't go somewhere with him or just spend time together because I had to work (I do a lot of my work from home) or had commitments to clients. I have made a promise to myself to use my assertive communication skills and tell people, "Thank you for asking me, but I have a commitment to my husband."

How can you say "no" in a way that honors what is important to you?

Exercise #17:
For each request you get, identify at least 3 different ways of saying "no": For example, a friend asks me to head up a volunteer committee at our local hospital.

1. Just say "no." "Thank you. I'm going to pass on that"

2. Gracious no: "Thank you for thinking of me for this important project, but my non-work time is already committed."

3. Family no: Thank you for thinking of me, but I have heavy family commitments over the next few months.

4. Better resource no: "I am sorry I don't have the time to help. Have you thought about Sara Smith?? She is a great organizer!

What other kinds of no's can you come up with?

1. _____

2. _____

3. _____

Exercise #18:

For the next week, try writing down various requests that are made of you. Then note your response. Is it difficult for you to say "no," even though you would like to?

Request: _____

My response : _____

Request: _____

My response: _____

Request: _____

My response : _____

Request: _____

My response: _____

Request: _____

My response: _____

Request: _____

My response: _____

There are many different ways to say "no". You may feel that you need time before giving an answer to a request. Simply saying, "Let me think about it" can give you the opportunity to make a sound decision and respond in a way that honors your needs as well as those of the person making the request.

MANAGING YOUR TIME

At the end of the day, do you ever feel as though you just rushed away an entire day? I have to admit that when I become focused on completing a project, I work from sunrise to sunset, anxiously trying to cram everything possible into every available minute. The great lesson about time management isn't mastering the art of cramming more into the day. It is about consciously experiencing every moment we are given. Right now my score on that skill would be about a C-, maybe a D+. What many of us still need to "get" at a deep level, is that life isn't about what happens when we complete that project, or get the house cleaned, or complete our "to do" list. Life is about what is happening now, one moment at a time.

As noted in Chapter Four, many of us experience the following problems:

- We are constantly rushing.
- We are focused on our unfinished business, rather than feeling peaceful.
- We tend to overcommit.
- We don't take time to play because we have too much work to do.
- We neglect family and friends because of our busy schedule (my downfall!).
- We spend most of our time completing our "to do" list, rather than doing the things we want to do.

Exercise #19:

Take a moment to circle those of the above problems that are true in your life. This will give you a frame of reference for whether you might benefit from better time management.

Exercise #20:

In deciding how we want to spend the time available to us, it is important to identify our priorities. A quick, but effective exercise to help you identify some of your priorities is to ask yourself, "What would I prioritize if I only had one more year to live? What do I value (i.e., family, friends, financial security, travel, creativity?) Who would I want to spend time with? What would I like to accomplish?"

1. _____

2. _____

3. _____

4. _____

When thinking about what's really important in our lives, we sometimes overlook big areas without thinking about it. For example, we often neglect to build in time for fun and play in our daily routine.

Exercise #21:

Consider the areas of your life listed below. For each one, answer this question: What is my main priority in this area of my life?

Professional: _____

Relationships: _____

Creative Activities: _____

Spiritual: _____

Volunteer/altruistic: _____

Health: _____

Take the list you just made and reorder it, putting the items in the order of their value to you, from greatest to least.

1. _____
2. _____
3. _____
4. _____
5. _____
6. _____

Exercise #22:

This next exercise will help you to determine how you actually use your time. Create a log of how you spend your time over a typical three-day period.

Day 1:

Activity: _____
6 A.M. _____
7 A.M. _____
8 A.M. _____
9 A.M. _____
10 A.M. _____
11 A.M. _____
12:00 Noon_____
1 P.M. _____
2 P.M _____
 3 P.M. _____
4 P.M. _____
5 P.M. _____
6 P.M. _____
7 P.M. _____
8 P.M. _____
9 P.M. _____
10 P.M _____

Day 2:

Activity: _____
6 A.M. _____
7 A.M. _____
8 A.M. _____
9 A.M. _____
10 A.M. _____

11 A.M. ———————————————
12:00 Noon———————————————
1 P.M. ———————————————
2 P.M ———————————————
3 P.M. ———————————————
4 P.M. ———————————————
5 P.M. ———————————————
6 P.M. ———————————————
7 P.M. ———————————————
8 P.M. ———————————————
9 P.M. ———————————————
10 P.M ———————————————

Day 3:

Activity: ———————————————
6 A.M. ———————————————
7 A.M. ———————————————
8 A.M. ———————————————
9 A.M. ———————————————
10 A.M. ———————————————
11 A.M. ———————————————
12:00 Noon———————————————
1 P.M. ———————————————
2 P.M ———————————————
3 P.M. ———————————————
4 P.M. ———————————————
5 P.M. ———————————————
6 P.M. ———————————————
7 P.M. ———————————————
8 P.M. ———————————————
9 P.M. ———————————————
10 P.M ———————————————

Ask yourself these questions:

1. Which of the activities in your log are consistent with your values and priorities? Which are not?
2. Are any of your activities in conflict with your values?
3. Are you neglecting any of your values and priorities?

Make a note of how you might change your daily activities to be more consistent with your values.

Focusing Your Time and Energy On Your Priorities

The concepts behind these next exercises were originally developed by Jennifer White, author of the excellent book entitled *Work Less, Make More*.

Exercise #23:

Take a look at the vision that you created in Chapter 7. Write down one or two priorities related to that vision that you would most like to accomplish in the next three to six months:

Example: Two priorities I would most like to accomplish in the next 3 to 6 months are:

1. Add 5 new local clients to my business.
2. Lose 2 inches on my hips.

Two priorities I would most like to accomplish in the next 3 to 6 months are:

1. _____

2. _____

Now, write down the three most important actions you must take to achieve those priorities—three big actions. This is called your *Power of Three.*

Example:

1. Build relationships with local businesses in need of my service.
2. Take sales training to improve close rate.
3. Establish and maintain an exercise program.

The three most important actions I can take to achieve my priorities are:

1. _____

2. _____

3. _____

The above list will center you on your main objectives for the week. They will drive the scheduling of daily and weekly activities that are geared to accomplish the three items on your list. Eighty percent of your time each week should be focused on the meetings, tasks and actions that support the three priorities you have identified as most important. When you build your schedule in this way, the most important work will get done each week. You can also do a Power of Three for work and a Power of Three for the rest of your life, if you prefer. The process is the same.

Most people spend very little time working on what matters most. Figure out what matters most to you and make choices in alignment with your vision, values, and priorities.

What To Do With the Rest

What do you do with all the other meetings, tasks, or actions that do not fit with the Power of Three? Some of it can be done in the remaining 20% of your time that is not allocated to the priority areas. The remainder will need to be delegated, automated, negotiated, or eliminated. A good acronym for these activities is DANE. Here is a suggestion for DANEing your tasks:

Exercise #24:

Pull out four sheets of paper. Label them as follows, with one header per sheet:

1. Delegate
2. Automate
3. Negotiate
4. Eliminate

Now allocate to one of the above DANE sheets the meetings, tasks and actions that don't fit with your Power of Three. Try to see how creative you can be in getting the work done. Look for ways that are a win for everyone. Think about automating as putting systems in place that will facilitate the work being done more efficiently. Consider training someone in your department to do the work that you do not enjoy but that they do! Win-win. Consider just saying "no"—eliminating it—and taking it off your plate. Learning to delegate, negotiate, eliminate, and automate wisely is an important part of time management. We have to realize that it is not only wise to ask for help, it is a necessity.

How will you use DANE to free up your time to achieve your most important goals? You may find it helpful to partner with a co-worker or friend to do the Power of Three and the DANE exercises. Often, we can become quite limited in our own thinking because we have been trying to balance a huge workload for a long time, or it seems too difficult to ask for help. Friends and co-workers can help you to be more ruthless in assigning your tasks. When someone else challenges us to come up with creative alternatives, the barriers break down and we can see additional possibilities.

When you notice that you are feeling rushed, stressed, and frustrated, take a moment to review and re-commit to your Power of Three and DANE strategies. In doing so, you will give yourself the gifts of health and peace of mind!

MAINTAINING A SENSE OF HUMOR

Research has shown that people are less affected by stress and adversity when they learn to use humor in their daily lives. I use the word "learn" to remind you that the use of humor is actually a learned skill that needs to be practiced frequently. Here are some exercises to help you get started practicing.

Exercise #25:

This exercise is designed to increase your awareness of your responses to stressful situations. Are your responses "doom and gloom" responses such as "My life is over." "I'll never be able to cope with this terrible situation." "I have so much to do that I'll never get it done." If your responses tend to "awfulize" situations you find yourself in, try this:

Stand in front of a mirror with a big smile on your face and say, "I can do this. I'll just take one step at a time, one day at a time, until it is done!"-or something to that effect.

Exercise #26:

Try greeting each new day by standing in front of a mirror, flinging your arms open wide, and saying: "Ta-Dah." This simple action gives your mind and your body the message that you believe in yourself and that you are ready for the day's challenges.

Exercise #27:

On your way into a meeting or stressful situation, try smile therapy. Smile for a minute, relax your jaw. Smile again. If you have a mirror, smile at yourself in front of the mirror. A smile has the effect of lifting our mood. Whenever I am feeling down and I have need to shift into a more productive frame of mind, I use smile therapy and it works every time.

Exercise #28:

Your goal is to increase humor in your life. Just as a smile on your face increases your ability to "lighten up," the following activities can also help you develop your sense of humor:

- Try reading some comic strips.
- Write down jokes that you enjoy.
- Watch the comedy channel television.
- Spend time with people who are fun and uplifting.
- Put on Groucho glasses—the ones with a big nose and bushy mustache and eyebrows—and wear them in public.

I tried the Groucho glasses while attending a clinical training at the Harvard Medial School Institute of Mind/Body Medicine. I was using public transportation to go from my hotel to the campus, and wore the glasses the entire trip. After my initial agony of embarrassment, I had a great time. Adults stared in shock and children laughed. No wonder kids have more fun.

Commit to having more fun in your life. If you seek out humorous experiences, you are sure to significantly enhance the quality of your life.

MANAGING YOUR FINANCES

In Chapter Four, we discussed five principles of financial management: To recap, they were:

- Know how much money you need to do what you want to do and have what you want to have.
- Live within your means.
- Build a reserve.
- Protect your most important assets (family, health, home, etc.).
- Make spending decisions based on your values.

Most of us have no idea how much money we need in order to do what we want to do and have what we truly want to have. It's easy to say we want to be millionaires, but is that really what we want? Or do we want to have enough money to buy that nice house in the country and a reliable car to get back and forth to town? It is critically important to know how much is enough for you.

Exercise #29:

Define what you really want to do and/or have in your life that requires money. Make an estimate of how much money you will need over and above what you are paying for that item now. In other words, if I want a new house that costs $200,000, but I own a house today that costs $100,000, the additional cost is $200,000 - 100,000 = $100,000. List all of your wants below. They may include a new car, a house, clothing, travel. Whatever it is, jot it down below and list the additional cost associated with the purchase. If you need more space to write, use another sheet. There is no limit on how many items you list. This is your list. See the example below.

List	Additional cost	Value met
1. Build reserve: 6months of living expenses	$12,000	Security
2. Health insurance, car ins, etc.	already covered	Health, family
3. New car - Toyota Camry	$400/month	Reliability
4. Redo kitchen	$20,000	Comfort, space

Total additional cost $32,000 plus $400/mo

Record Yours Here:

	List	Additional cost	Value met
1.			
2.			
3.			
4.			

This is a rough estimate of the total additional savings you will need in order to have what you want to have and do what you want to do. You can now begin to plan for how to create that amount. You can get there many different ways. How will you do it? Where will you spend less? How might you make more? How could you invest to grow your assets?

Take a look at where you are spending your money today and what you have to show for it. Look back at your spending patterns. What have you spent your money on? How much went into your car? Home? Food? Clothes? What was the total amount? Are you satisfied with what you have or did with all that money? Was the spending in alignment with what is truly important to you? If not, what areas do you need to adjust?

Purchase/spending	Cost	Why bought
1. New play clothes	$ 600	Feeling bad about myself
2. Mortgage on 3500 sq. ft house	$3300/month	Prestige of neighborhood
3. Expensive dinners (15)	$1500/month	Don't like job
4. ———————	————	——————
5. ———————	————	——————

List yours:

Purchase/spending	Cost	Why bought
1. ———————	————	——————
2. ———————	————	——————
3. ———————	————	——————
4. ———————	————	——————
5. ———————	————	——————

Many people find that this simple analysis helps them put their values and priorities into context. If what you most want to have or do is in front of you and you know the savings goal required, you are much more likely to achieve it. Further, when people review their past spending, they often find that much of it was not in alignment with what they most want to have or do. So, this process can simply highlight where your money is going and help you redirect it to where it matters most.

If you are spending money because you don't like your job, you may want to consider working with a career coach to find something that you enjoy more. In the short term, that may not create a financial savings, but in the long term it will benefit you in many ways. Before making any financial changes, contact a financial advisor to put together a plan so you can make the best use of your money. Consider additional means to earn more money. Read books. Invest. Build your reserve so that you get the benefit of compound interest over time. Live and spend in alignment with your values.

NETWORKING EFFECTIVELY:

The world is full of people who want to connect and accomplish something. Networking is the best way I know to make the connections. What better way to do it than to find someone else with similar or complementary goals?

Networking is a skill that can be built. You can build it through organizations such as the chamber of commerce, or you can join formal networking organizations such as Business Network International or eWomen Network. David Alexander, Executive Director of the Regional Office of Business Network International in Atlanta, shared these tools which dramatically increase your networking connections. These exercises are reprinted with permission from Ivan Misner, Ph.D., author of Business by Referral: A Sure-Fire Way to Generate New Business.

Exercise #30:

Start identifying people in the various categories shown below. Use these sheets as you would use a Roladex file, referring to them frequently whenever you need to tap into your "people resources."

Your Information Network

1. People who are trying to achieve the same things you want to achieve:

	Name	Address	Phone
1.	_____	_____	_____
2.	_____	_____	_____
3.	_____	_____	_____

2. People who are currently in the business or profession you are in or want to enter:

Name	Address	Phone
1. _____	_____	_____
2. _____	_____	_____
3. _____	_____	_____

3. People who were in the business or profession you are in or want to enter:

Name	Address	Phone
1. _____	_____	_____
2. _____	_____	_____
3. _____	_____	_____

4. People who write or produce books, tapes, or videos in your industry or specialty:

Name	Address	Phone
1. _____	_____	_____
2. _____	_____	_____
3. _____	_____	_____

5. People who regulate, audit, or monitor others in your field:

Name	Address	Phone
1. _____	_____	_____
2. _____	_____	_____
3. _____	_____	_____

6. People who train others in your field:

      Name   Address   Phone

  1. _____ _____ _____

  2. _____ _____ _____

  3. _____ _____ _____

7. People who advise or consult with people in your field:

      Name   Address   Phone

  1. _____ _____ _____

  2. _____ _____ _____

  3. _____ _____ _____

8. Members of trade, business, or professional organizations in your field:

      Name   Address   Phone

  1. _____ _____ _____

  2. _____ _____ _____

  3. _____ _____ _____

Your Referral Network

1. People in your contact sphere:

      Name   Address   Phone

  1. _____ _____ _____

  2. _____ _____ _____

  3. _____ _____ _____

2. Current or former clients:

    Name   Address   Phone

    1. _____   _____   _____
    2. _____   _____   _____
    3. _____   _____   _____

3. People who get more business when you get more business.

    Name   Address   Phone

    1. _____   _____   _____
    2. _____   _____   _____
    3. _____   _____   _____

4. People you do business with other than your supplies and vendors:

    Name   Address   Phone

    1. _____   _____   _____
    2. _____   _____   _____
    3. _____   _____   _____

5. Current or former staff members, part time or full time:

    Name   Address   Phone

    1. _____   _____   _____
    2. _____   _____   _____
    3. _____   _____   _____

6. People you have given referrals to:

   Name   Address   Phone

   1. _____   _____   _____

   2. _____   _____   _____

   3. _____   _____   _____

7. Anyone who has given you referrals:

   Name   Address   Phone

   1. _____   _____   _____

   2. _____   _____   _____

   3. _____   _____   _____

8. Other members of business referral groups:

   Name   Address   Phone

   1. _____   _____   _____

   2. _____   _____   _____

   3. _____   _____   _____

Maintain A Lifestyle of Self-Care 10

Once you are on a path to achieving the success you want in your life, you will want to insure that you maintain a lifestyle of self-care that will support that success, promote health, and renew energy. We have previously discussed several ways that you can care for yourself to enhance your overall sense of well-being. Chapter Five was the theory. This chapter is the nuts and bolts!

As you will recall, some of the most important aspects of self-care are:
- relaxation on a regular basis,
- regular exercise,
- maintaining a healthy diet,
- developing social support, and
- connecting with your spiritual nature.

Techniques for eliciting the relaxation response were discussed in Chapter Eleven (Continuously Acquire Life Skills for Effectiveness.) Strategies for developing an exercise program, maintaining a healthy diet, developing social support, and connecting with your spiritual nature are provided in this chapter.

A Word of Caution

Before starting even a mild exercise program, see your doctor—especially if you are out of shape, have had recent surgery, have high blood pressure, or have any injury such as a torn ligament in your knee which might be stressed by exercise. If you have any history of cardiovascular problems, the President's Council suggests a physician's checkup including an electrocardiogram.

REGULAR EXERCISE

When you are starting an exercise program, if maximum well-being is your goal, a wise choice is exercise that increases your cardiovascular endurance. Exercising at a range of 50 to 60% of the heart's maximal capacity results in definite cardiovascular benefits.

Keep in mind that your goal is not to obtain the maximal capacity, but to select a target heart rate that will provide the benefits you desire. Your target heart rate is based on your maximal heart rate. The best way to calculate your maximal heart rate without actually exercising is to subtract your age from the number 220. For example, if you are 40 years old, your maximal heart rate would be:

$$220 - 40 = 180$$

You now want to determine your target heart rate, the heart rate you wish to achieve during exercise. While earlier experts recommended a target rate of at least 65—80% of your maximal heart rate—opinion has shifted. The recommended minimum target heart rate during exercise is now suggested to be 50 to 60% of your heart's maximum capacity. Your target heart rate can be determined by multiplying your maximal heart rate (see above example) by the percentage you have selected as your targeted heart rate. It is wise to involve your physician in this decision. If you and your physician have chosen 60% as your target heart rate, and you are 40 years old, the formula would look like this:

$$180 \text{ (maximal heart rate)} \times .60 = 108$$

Thus, 108 is your target heart rate. To check your heart rate during exercise, take your pulse immediately upon interrupting exercise. Count your pulse for 6 seconds and multiply by 10 to get the rate per minute.

Exercise #1: Finding a Good Fit
Several activities and sports are listed below. Some are aerobic (they use the oxygen your body takes in through breathing); some are anaerobic (they use more than the oxygen your body takes in through breathing). Circle a few of both kinds that you think you might enjoy.

Aerobic:	Aerobic (continued)	Anerobic
Jogging	In-line skating	Baseball/Softball
Walking	Hiking	Volleyball
Soccer	Cycling	Weight lifting
Basketball	Cross-country skiing	Push-ups
Swimming	Aerobics videos	Sit-ups
Horseback riding		Tennis

If you think of your own ideas for exercise, write them down below.

_____

_____

Exercise #2: Find Your Target Heart Rate

Now that you have identified a few ways you would enjoy moving your body and increasing your heart rate, the next step is to determine what your target heart rate for exercise should be. In order to determine your target heart rate, you first need to determine your maximal exercise capacity. This is defined as the most exercise you can do before fatigue makes you stop. The heart rate you obtain with maximal exercise is your maximal heart rate.

309

Step 1: Calculate your maximal heart rate by subtracting your age from 220. For example, if you are 40 years old, your maximal heart rate would be:

$$220 - 40 = 180$$

My maximal heart rate is:

Step 2: Take that number and multiply it by 60 percent (your maximal heart rate) x .60 =

(target heart rate) _____

Now you have a goal heart rate to shoot for in your workouts! One hint: You don't need to reach this heart rate the first time you work out. In fact, if you do, you'll probably huff and puff so hard that you will never be able to keep it up. Make your target heart rate a goal to work up to. Listen to your body while you exercise. You should be able to think straight and even talk while exercising. Use good judgment!

Getting Started

Don't start by working out every single day. A great beginning expectation is three times a week, but if that's too hard, don't do it. Remember that short-term goals should be baby steps toward your long-term goals. The long-term goal here is establishing an exercise routine. So, make lots of little steps to help you along the way. Don't forget, it's helpful to have a buddy to exercise with you. Not only will he or she make the walk or swim or sit-ups more fun, that person will hold you accountable. If you can join an established group, that might be a good option. Not only will your fun and consistency increase, but you'll probably make some new friends, too!

Exercise #3: Exercise Buddies

People I could contact to exercise with me:

1. _____

2. _____

3. _____

4. _____

Exercise #4: Basic Goal Setting

Here's a basic goal-setting exercise to help you stay on track with your new exercise program. Your long-term goals don't have to be fitness-related. Your goal can be to get proficient at volleyball, and fitness can become a fringe benefit.

1. Long Term Goal:

_____

2. Short Term Goals I'll accomplish along the way:
   A. _____
   B. _____
   C. _____
   D. _____

Yoga:

For a stress reducer, I enjoy gentle yoga stretches. They are relaxing and help relieve tension. Yoga is a very good form of exercise to use during warm-up and cool-down. Yoga stretches and tones muscles, and, as a fringe benefit, provides you the opportunity to elicit the relaxation response through mindfulness.

If you would enjoy an audio-tape to guide you through some yoga stretching exercises, there are many available at Amazon.com or your local bookstore, or you can try my *"Stretch and Renew"* tape. This tape can be found on my website, www.donnadaisy.com.

Suggestions

If you are just getting started in an exercise program, the following suggestions may be helpful:

- Choose an activity that you enjoy.
- Select an exercise program that is realistic.
- Include warm-up stretches before any exercise.
- Include exercise in your daily schedule.
- Consider an exercise buddy or group for motivation.
- Reward yourself when you achieve one of your goals.
- If you feel pain, you're working too hard.
- If you get hurt, stop until you have healed.
- Find ways to continue increasing your physical activity in your everyday life.

Exercise #5: Reward Yourself Along The Way

Here's the part everyone likes—rewards! When you complete some of your short-term goals, reward all your hard work with something worthy. For instance, if you're really enjoying in-line skating and you complete your second week in a row of three exercise periods a week, reward yourself with a trip to a fitness store for a new exercise outfit or that much-needed water bottle you can strap to your waist! Make your rewards fun and gratifying, and design them to help you continue on toward your long- term goals. You can plan how you are going to reward yourself by using this format:

When I complete this short-term goal (fill in goal here)

_____

I'll reward myself with the following:

_____

MAINTAINING A HEALTHY DIET

When life seems incredibly stressful, many of us find it tempting to try to reduce stress by eating. While we may get temporary satisfaction from eating, we often pay a high price for this relief including:

- weight gain
- lowered self-esteem
- thinking that is less clear because the blood is directed away from the brain and concentrated in the stomach
- upset digestive system

Many of us struggle with finding a healthy balance of essential nutrients and caloric intake. It is much too easy to run by a fast-food restaurant or grab snacks at home to "tide us over." As a part of creating and maintaining a healthy lifestyle, we need to take a look at our own eating habits. The USDA Food Guide Pyramid is a good guide for conveying information about a healthy diet. The following information is a good guide for where our dietary emphasis should be placed. The information below represents servings per day. A serving consists of ½ cup.

- Bread, cereal, rice, and pasta: 6-8 servings
- Vegetables: 3-5 servings
- Fruit: 2-4 servings
- Milk, yogurt, cheese: 2-3 servings
- Meat, poultry, fish, dry beans, eggs, and nuts: 2-3 servings
- Fats, oils, and sugar: Use sparingly

As you move toward healthier eating, it is helpful to observe daily patterns and make minimal but consistent changes towards healthy nutrition. The first step is to become aware of your eating habits.

Exercise #6: Discover Your Negative Eating Habits

Check the habits that apply to you:

_____1. I use coffee to "get going."

_____2. I eat snacks or pastries when I'm in a hurry.

_____3. I drink coffee throughout the day to "keep going."

_____4. I often eat fast foods.

_____5. I often renew my energy in the afternoon with sugary snacks.

_____6. I often fix a frozen dinner rather than prepare a nutritious meal.

_____7. I often reward myself with high calorie snacks in the evening.

_____8. I have trouble falling asleep because of my late-night snacking.

_____9. When I don't get much sleep, I rely on coffee as an "eye opener."

_____10. Add other examples of your own.

Exercise #7: Identifying Negative Food Choices

Many of us are in the habit of making negative or unwise food choices, both for meals and for snacks. By completing this exercise, you can identify negative food choices you may be making and begin to make changes toward healthful eating.

Think back over the past day. What meals and snacks did you eat?

_____

Which of these things were healthy, and which were not so healthy?

_____

Were you really hungry when you ate?

_____

If not, why do you think you ate?

_____

Changes You Can Make

If you are eating in response to stress, some changes you might make are:

- Start the day with a nutritious breakfast.
- Keep healthy snacks available.
- Eat more fruits and vegetables.
- Drink lots of water to reduce snacking.
- Avoid or cut down on caffeine, black teas, soft drinks, and chocolate.
- If you work outside the home, prepare a nutritious lunch and "brown bag" it.
- For lunches or snacks, consider choosing low-fat, protein-rich foods. These will increase motivation, reaction time, and alertness.

- Make rich meals and desserts a treat rather than a daily habit.
- If you have a desire for sweet snacks, keep naturally sweetened cookies available.
- When having lunch at work, use the office microwave to cook a low-fat entrée.

When you are tempted to turn to food as a coping strategy, an alternative strategy is to engage in a tension-relieving activity instead. Some ideas are:

- Take several deep breaths.
- Go for a walk for as long as time allows.
- Do some slow, deep stretches.
- Tense and relax all your muscles three times.
- Call a friend to reconnect.
- When possible, get outside and breathe some fresh air.

SOCIAL SUPPORT

Relationships in the form of social support are good for our health and even our productivity. Research has shown that support groups, family, friends, and co-workers can often provide the supportive network needed for healing and for stress reduction. Talking with others gives us a chance to let off steam as well as to hear a different perspective. It is my belief that we are here to support and care for one another. Relationships characterized by love, warmth, forgiveness, acceptance, and effective communication are among the important foundational pieces for our ability to overcome adversity and achieve the success we want in our lives.

We all know the value of feeling connected and feeling loved. In the end, it isn't what we did for a living, or how much money we made that we will want to be remembered for. What most of us want at a very deep level is for people to know we loved them and were there for them, and we will want to feel loved and supported by them in return.

When we are under stress and pressure, high quality relationships with family, friends, co-workers and professionals can provide the support we need to rekindle our energies and hopes. High quality relationships are those that give you energy, not those that drain you. High quality relationships give you deep connections with others. They give you support. They inspire you. They challenge you to be your best.

Many of us have a lack of high quality relationships in our lives. Sometimes family members aren't able to give the love and support we need. Sometimes our relationships with others are unhealthy, and drain us of energy. That's why you may need to consciously build the social support system you want in your life.

Exercise #8: Build Your Support System
This exercise will help you identify the social support you already have in place in your life, and begin to identify areas in which you need to enlarge your circle of support:

List those people who listen to you, support you, challenge you, and energize you and how often you engage with each of them in a quality way.

Family Members:

_____

_____

Friends:

_____

_____

Co-Workers:

_____

_____

Professionals:

_____

_____

Other Community Members:

_____

_____

B. Now, ask yourself:

"In what ways do I need to expand my social support system?"

_____

"Are there people I would like to connect with on a deeper level? If so, who?"

_____

"Do I have unhealthy relationships in my life that I need to get rid of? If so, which ones?"

_____

_____

"Am I spending too much time with people who are not very important to me or who don't feed my soul? If so, who are they and what will I do differently?"

_____

_____

"What are the qualities I want in my social support members?" (i.e. good listener, warm, caring, non-judgmental but willing to challenge me, share my values)

_____

_____

"Are there people I want to start including in my suport network? If so, who?"

_____

_____

Now, start taking action. Consciously begin creating ways to develop deeper and more meaningful relationships with those whom you have identified. A good place to start is by acknowledging and expressing your appreciation of others. Give someone a call. Write a note acknowledging a kind act or a good job someone did. Perhaps the slogan "Reach out and touch someone" is the best guideline of all for starting to build and strengthen your social support system.

CONNECTING WITH YOUR SPIRITUAL NATURE

Spirituality means different things to different people. For some, spirituality is represented by a sense of meaning and purpose in life. For others, it is a sense of connection to a power greater than ourselves.

Our spirituality often manifests in the form of a small voice within us that is always trying to get our attention, but all too often is overpowered by the noisiness of our busy lives. I call that voice our inner wisdom. The following are some strategies for developing a personal spiritual practice that fits into your life and allows you to connect with your inner wisdom, honor it, and nurture it.

Exercise #9:

One way of connecting with your inner wisdom is to simply take time to listen to that still small voice within you. Some people refer to that voice as your intuition. Take a moment and recall a time when you had a strong feeling that doing something wasn't in your best interest. Write this experience down:

_____

_____

Now, think about a time when you absolutely knew without a doubt that it was the time to take a particular action. Describe that experience:

_____

_____

_____

Did you take that action? It has been my experience that the more we learn to trust that inner voice, the wiser our actions become. My partner, Abby, called me regarding a major decision she had to make in her life. She had been offered a significant amount of money to take on a particular project, but her inner wisdom was telling her that if she took on the project, in addition to the work load she already carried, she would quickly be worn out and burnt out. Taking on this project would mean making a choice between self-care and time with her husband, or accepting the tempting lucrative opportunity. Fortunately, Abby was well tuned in to that voice within her, and was able to act on its wisdom. Even though she was sorry to turn down that big project, over the next few months, she was able to build her practice steadily and achieve tremendous success, while also taking time to care for herself and for those she loves.

Exercise #10:

Create and maintain a regular practice of checking in with your inner wisdom. You may find that you are better able to connect with that inner voice when you engage in a particular activity. Some activities that my coaching clients enjoy are engaging in prayer, taking walks in nature, doing sitting meditations, reading from a particularly inspiring book, or listening to inspirational audiotapes. Some people use their quiet time to write their thoughts in a journal. Many of my clients get in touch with their spiritual nature by asking themselves questions such as:

"What do I value most in my life?"

"Am I living those values?"

"Whom do I love and have I loved well?"

"What do I need to do to nourish my soul?"

Take a moment to think about some ways that you can honor your spiritual well-being on a regular basis. Write them down here.

_____

_____

Next, think about which time of day or evening is best for your daily spiritual practice. For me, early morning is the time that I am most able to quiet and clear my mind. Others enjoy late afternoon, or ending the day with quiet time. Write down the time that is best for your spiritual practice.

_____

_____

Remember, your spirituality and your sense of meaning and purpose in life are the sources of great energy. They are powerful motivators toward accomplishment. Even more important, they are a great source of satisfaction in your life, as they can be the basis of an overall sense of personal and spiritual well-being.

References & Resources

Bandura, A. "Self-efficacy Mechanisms governing the Motivational Effects of Goal Systems," *Journal of Personality and Social Psychology, 45,* 1017-1028.

Benson, H., and Klipper, M. *The Relaxation Response.* New York: Avon Books, 1976.

Benson, H., and Stuart, E. *The Wellness Book.* New York: Simon & Schuster, 1992.

Benson, H., with Stark, M. *Timeless Healing.* New York: Fireside, 1997.

Borysenko, J. *Minding the Body, Mending the Mind.* Reading, MA: Addison-Wesley, 1987.

Borysenko, J. *Inner Peace for Busy People.* Carlsbad, CA: Hay House, Inc. 2001.

Brandon, N. *The Six Pillars of Self-esteem.* New York: Bantam Books, 1994.

Brandon, N. *Taking Responsibility.* New York: Fireside, 1996.

REFERENCES AND RESOURCES

Brandon, N. *The Art of Living Consciously.* New York: Fireside, 1996.

Burns, D. *The Feeling Good Handbook.* New York: William Morrow and Company, 1989.

Burns, D. *Ten Days to Self-Esteem.* New York: William Morrow and Company, Inc., 1993.

Cameron, J. *The Artist's Way: A Spiritual Path to Higher Creativity.* New York: Penguin Putnam, Inc., 1992.

Chopra, D. *The Seven Spiritual Laws of Success.* San Rafael, CA: Amber-Allen Publishing and New World Library, 1994.

Carlson, R. *Don't Sweat the Small Stuff - - and It's All Small Stuff.* New York: Hyperion, 1997.

Cohen, A. *A Deep Breath of Life.* Carlsbad, CA:, Hay House, Inc., 1996.

Conners, R., Smith, T., Hickman, C. *The OZ Principle: Getting Results Through Individudal and Organizational Accountability.* Englewood Cliffs, CA: Prentice Hall, 1994.

Covey, S. *The Seven Habits of Highly Effective People.* New York: Fireside Books, 1989.

Daisy, D. *How to Have a Really Good Life—and Reduce Stress While You're at It.* Self-Published, 1999.

Dossey, L. *Healing Words.* New York: Harper-Collins, 1993.

Dweck, C. "Self-theories and Goals: Their Role in Motivation, personality, and Development." In R. A. Dienstbier (Ed.), *Perspectives on Motivation.* Nebraska Symposium on Motivation. Lincoln: University of Nebraska Press, 1991.

Dyer, W. *Real Magic.* New York: Harper-Collins, 1992.

Foundation for Inner Peace. *A Course in Miracles.* Text, workbook, and workbook for teachers. Farmingdale, NY: Foundation for Inner Peace, 1975.

Frankl, V. *Man's Search for Meaning.* New York: Washington Square Press. 1959.

Gawain, S. *Creative Visualizations.* New York: Bantam Books, 1979.

H. H. the Dalai Lama, and Cutler, H. D. *The Art of Happiness.* New York: Riverhead Books, 1998.

Hafen, B., Karren, K., Frandsen, K., and Smith, N. L. *Mind/Body Health.* Needham Heights, MA: Allyn & Bacon, 1996.

REFERENCES AND RESOURCES

Hanh, T. N. *The Miracle of Mindfulness! A Manual on Meditation.* Boston: Beacon Press, 1976.

Jampolsky, G. *Love is Letting Go of Fear.* Berkeley, CA: Celestial Arts, 1979.

Jones, L. B. *The Path: Creating Your Mission Statement for Work and for Life.* New York: Hyperion, 1996.

Kabat-Zinn, J. *Full Catastrophe Living: Using the Wisdom of Your Body and Mind to Face S t r e s s , Pain and Illness.* New York: Delacorte Press, 1990.

Kobasa, S.C., Maddi, S.R. and Pucretti, M.C. Personality and Exercise as Buffers in the Stress-Illness Relationship. *Journal of Behavioral Medicine, 5,* 391-404. (Also referenced as Suzanne Oullette.)

Langer, E. *Mindfulness.* Reading, MA: Addison-Wesley, 1989.

Misner, I.R. and Davis, R. *Business by Referral: A Sure-Fire Way to Generate New Business.* Austin: Bard Press, 1997.

Northrup, C. *Women's Bodies, Women's Wisdom.* New York: Bantam Books, 1998.

Levine, S. *A Gradual Awakening.* New York: Anchor Books, 1979.

Locke, E.A.and Latham, G.P. *A Theory of Goal Setting and Task Performance.* Englewood Cliffs, NJ: Prentice Hall,1990.

Maslow, A. H. *Motivation and Personality.* New York: Harper & Row, 1970.

O'Hara, V. *Wellness at Work: Building Resilience to Job Stress.* Oakland, CA: New Harbinger Publications, 1995.

Orman, S. *The 9 Steps to Financial Freedom.* New York: Three Rivers Press, 1997.

Oullette, S. See reference under Kobasa, S.

Pransky, G. *The Relationship Handbook.* New York: McGraw Hill, 1992.

Richardson, C. *Take Time for Your Life.* New York: Broadway Books, 1999.

Sawi, B. *Coming Up for Air.* New York: Hyperion, 2000.

Seligman, M.E.P., and Maier. "Failure to Escape Shock." *Journal of Experimental Psychology,* 1974.

Seligman, M. *Helplessness: On Depression, Development and Death.* New York: W.H. Freeman & Co, 1975.

REFERENCES AND RESOURCES

Seligman, M.E.P. *Learned Optimism.* New York: Alfred A. Knopf, 1990.

Siegel, B. *Love, Medicine and Miracles.* New York: Harper & Row, 1986.

Stoltz, P. *The Adversity Quotient.* New York: John Wiley & Sons, Inc., 1997.

White, J. *Work Less, Make More.* New York: John Wiley & Sons, Inc., 1998.

Williamson, M.A. *A Return to Love.* New York: Harper-Collins, 1993.

Williamson, M. *Illuminata: A Return to Prayer.* New York: Riverhead Books, 1994.

About the Authors

Donna Daisy Ph.D.

As a success coach, author, and professional speaker, Donna believes that the best way to predict the future is to create it. Ten years as Executive Director of a large non-profit agency combined with twenty-five years experience as a therapist, counselor and workshop leader have provided the background for what Donna does best—helping people create their future.

Donna's professional training, life experience and doctoral studies focusing on human motivation, goal setting, achievement and life satisfaction provide the fundamental, research-based foundation for her powerful Model for Success presented in **RISE ABOVE IT**. Interviews with dozens of people about what works for them in their lives, plus the wisdom that comes from many lessons learned while stumbling, falling, getting up and trying again, have provided the basis for the strategies found in this book. In her books, tapes and workshops, Donna encourages others to embrace their personal power, make life changing choices, and take the necessary action to create the results they want in their lives.

Donna lives in Greenville, Illinois with her husband Charles, and her favorite four-legged companion, Abby.

Abby Donnelly

Abby Donnelly is the President and Founder of Strategic Choices, Inc., a coaching and training company dedicated to delivering high-impact results.

Her professional experience includes over 14 years as a business leader, internal consultant and executive coach at Procter & Gamble. Abby's greatest strength is in her ability to help her clients define and clarify their business goals and to provide practical guidance, tools, and methodology to help them achieve more than they ever thought possible.

As a senior trainer and curriculum designer for two coach training programs and a contributor to the book, *Drive Your People Wild Without Driving Them Crazy™* by Jennifer White, Abby brings a wealth of experience and expertise to the strategies and exercises found in RISE ABOVE IT.

Abby has been married for 13 years to her husband and best friend, Jim. She enjoys dancing, dining out, walking and reading.

More Information

For more information, to give your feedback, or to subscribe to Donna Daisy's online newsletter, please visit her website at **www.donnadaisy.com** or send email to **donna@donnadaisy.com**.

Book Orders:

Order online from Trafford Publishers at: **www.trafford.com/robots/02-0172.html**

Contact:
      TRAFFORD PUBLISHERS
      2333 Government St,. Suite 6E
      Victoria, BC, Canada V8T 4P4
      250-383-6864
      Toll-free 1-888-232-4444 (US and Canada)
      Fax 250-383-6804

ISBN 1553693590